# COMP[illegible]AL INTE[illegible]CE

# COMPUTATIONAL INTELLIGENCE

**D. Menaka**
Associate Professor,
Dept of CSE, Sathyabama Institute
of Science and Technology

**J. Jeyshri**
Associate Professor,
Dept of CSE, Sathyabama Institute
of Science and Technology

KHANNA BOOK
PUBLISHING CO. (P) Ltd.
4C/4344, Ansari Road, Darya Ganj,
New Delhi, India

Sathyabama Institute of
Science and Technology
Jeppiaar Nagar, Rajiv Gandhi Salai,
Chennai, Tamilnadu, India

Dear Readers,

To prevent the piracy, this book is secured with HIGH SECURITY HOLOGRAM on the front title cover. In case you don't find the hologram on the front cover title, please write us to at contact@khannabooks.com or whatsapp us at +91-99109 09320 and avail special gift voucher for yourself.

Specimen of Hologram on front Cover title: 

Moreover, there is a SPECIAL DISCOUNT COUPON for you with EVERY HOLOGRAM.

How to avail this SPECIAL DISCOUNT:

Step 1: Scratch the hologram
Step 2: Under the scratch area, your "coupon code" is available
Step 3: Logon to www.khannabooks.com
Step 4: Use your "coupon code" in the shopping cart and get your copy at a special discount
Step 5: Enjoy your reading!

Thanks,
Khanna Publishing House

**ISBN:** 978-93-55382-76-4

**COMPUTATIONAL INTELLIGENCE**
*by* **D. Menaka | J. Jeyshri**

**First Edition:** 2025

To view complete list of books, please scan the QR Code:

*Published by:*
**Khanna Book Publishing Co. (P) Ltd.**
CIN: U22110DL1998PTC095547

Visit us at: www.khannabooks.com
Write us at: contact@khannabooks.com

Printed in Bharat.

# Preface

Computational Intelligence (CI) has emerged as a powerful paradigm in solving complex real-world problems by leveraging techniques inspired by natural intelligence. As the demand for intelligent systems grows, the field continues to evolve, integrating concepts from artificial intelligence, machine learning, neural networks, evolutionary computing, and fuzzy logic.

This book aims to provide a comprehensive overview of computational intelligence, offering insights into its theoretical foundations, methodologies, and practical applications. It is designed to cater to students, researchers, and professionals seeking to understand and implement intelligent computational models for diverse problem-solving scenarios.

The chapters cover fundamental principles, key algorithms, and recent advancements, ensuring a balance between theoretical knowledge and hands-on implementation. By exploring real-world case studies and examples, readers will gain a deeper appreciation of how CI techniques are applied across various domains, including healthcare, finance, robotics, and optimization.

Our objective is to present a structured yet accessible guide that encourages curiosity and innovation in computational intelligence. We hope that this work will serve as a valuable resource for anyone looking to harness the power of intelligent computing to address modern challenges.

# Contents

1

# Artificial Intelligence

UNIT

## RATIONALE

Artificial Intelligence (AI) is transforming various fields, making it a crucial area of study. This chapter explores AI's relevance in automating tasks, enhancing decision-making, and solving complex problems. It covers AI applications in healthcare, finance, education, and industry, emphasizing its role in improving efficiency and innovation. The ethical considerations, challenges, and future advancements in AI are also discussed. Understanding AI is essential for adapting to technological advancements and leveraging its benefits responsibly. This chapter provides insights into AI's impact on society, preparing readers to engage with AI-driven developments in their respective fields.

## 1.1 INTRODUCTION

Artificial intelligence (AI) is a machine's ability to mimic human actions in problem solving and performing activities that require complex thought processes. This often involves identifying aspects of human cognition and translating them into algorithms that computers can process. The level of flexibility and efficiency in these approaches varies based on specific requirements, influencing how "intelligent" the system appears. While AI is commonly associated with computer science, it also has strong connections to other disciplines such as mathematics, psychology, cognitive science, biology, and philosophy. Advancing AI development relies on integrating knowledge from these diverse fields, bringing us closer to creating truly intelligent artificial systems.

> **AI has the ability to improve its own computational algorithms. Through processes like neural architecture search, AI systems can discover and optimize algorithms that outperform human-designed ones in certain tasks, such as image recognition or natural language processing.**
>
> *Interesting Facts*

AI presently includes a vast array of subfields, ranging from general-purpose domains like vision and logical reasoning to specialized jobs like creating poetry, detecting illnesses, playing chess, and proving mathematical theorems. Scientists from other disciplines frequently make a gradual transition to artificial intelligence, where they acquire the terminology and tools necessary to organize and automate the cognitive processes, they have been engaged in throughout their life. Similar to this, AI researchers are free to adapt their techniques to any field of human intellectual pursuit. It is a really worldwide field in this way.

AI has eight definitions that are arranged in two dimensions. While the definitions at the bottom deal with conduct, the ones at the top deal with cognitive processes and reasoning.

## Understanding Intelligence and AI

Intelligence consists of several key components, including:

- Reasoning
- Learning
- Problem-Solving
- Perception
- Linguistic **Intelligence**

AI leverages various tools such as probability models, economic principles, logic, search algorithms, and mathematical optimization techniques. Branches such as computer science, mathematics, neuroscience, and artificial psychology all come together to form the singular field that is known as artificial intelligence.

In this case, the analyze is grasping the behavior and thinking of a person. This is achieved by developing machines with human-like intelligence and capabilities, including robotics, facial recognition, and natural language processing. While AI is currently most commonly applied in computing, healthcare, and the military, it is expected to become increasingly integrated into everyday life.

### 1.1.1 Applications of Artificial Intelligence

Many theories suggest that AI may eventually surpass human intelligence due to its ability to learn rapidly, process vast amounts of data efficiently, and make quicker decisions. However, despite its advancements, AI still has limitations. For instance, machines struggle with physical tasks such as operating heavy equipment or driving in extreme conditions.

- **Applications of Artificial Intelligence:** AI has numerous real-world uses in a wide range of sectors and fields, such as:
- **Healthcare:** AI is utilized in drug development, medical diagnostics, and disease prediction.
- **Finance:** AI supports financial forecasts, fraud detection, and credit rating.
- **Retail:** Supply chain management, pricing optimization, and product recommendations are all aided by AI.
- **Manufacturing:** AI supports production optimization, predictive maintenance, and quality control.
- **Transportation:** AI is applied to route planning, traffic forecasting, and driverless cars.
- **Customer service:** AI-driven chatbots are employed to provide customer service, respond to often requested queries, and manage straightforward tasks.
- **Security:** AI is utilized for threat analysis in cybersecurity, intrusion detection, and facial recognition.
- **Marketing:** Sentiment analysis, customer segmentation, and targeted advertising are all made with AI.
- **Education:** Intelligent tutoring programs, adaptive assessment, and tailored learning are all made possible by AI.

### 1.1.2 Significance of Artificial Intelligence

Artificial intelligence aims to develop intelligent expert systems that can educate, explain, illustrate concepts, and provide guidance to users. It enables computers to address complex problems in a manner similar to human reasoning by converting them into computationally efficient methods. One of AI's key advantages is its ability to enhance efficiency by automating time-consuming and labor-intensive tasks. Additionally, AI improves decision-making by analyzing large volumes of data and generating valuable insights, particularly in critical industries such as finance, healthcare, and logistics. Accuracy is another major benefit, as AI processes data swiftly and precisely, reducing the likelihood of human errors and enhancing the quality and reliability of outcomes. Furthermore, AI enhances personalization by tailoring interactions and recommendations based on some individual preferences and behaviors. Beyond these applications, AI also plays a crucial role in advancing scientific discovery by uncovering new information that might be difficult or impossible for humans to obtain, contributing to breakthroughs in fields like astronomy, genetics, and pharmaceutical research.

## 1.2 FOUNDATIONS OF AI

### 1.2.1 AI Methods

There are four different methods to artificial intelligence, and they are as follows:

1. **Behaving humanely (The Turing Test method):** Alan Turing created this method. The idea behind this method is that if a human interrogator asks some written questions and is unable to determine whether the written answers are from a computer or a human, then the computer has passed the test.
2. **Cognitive Modeling Approach:** Assessing whether a computer thinks like a human is the goal of the cognitive modeling approach, which is sometimes known as "thinking humanly."
3. **Thinking in order "the laws of thought" techniques:** This method aims to find out how advanced the logic capabilities of the computer system and its ability to reason is.
4. **Acting traditionally (The sensible agent approach):** This method seeks to establish if the computer functions logically and take rational decisions.

#### Machine Learning Approach

This method teaches machines to learn from data and gradually get better at certain jobs. It is extensively utilized in fields including recommender systems, natural language processing, and picture and audio recognition.

#### Evolutionary Approach

This method draws inspiration from biology's natural selection process. It entails coming up with and testing a lot of different approaches to an issue, then picking and merging the best ones to produce a fresh batch of solutions.

Many neural networks that are based on the composition and operations of the human brain are constructed using the neural networks technique. Tasks like pattern recognition, prediction, and decision-making can be handled by neural networks. Fuzzy logic is a method of reasoning with imprecise and uncertain data, which is frequently encountered in real-world scenarios. In fields like industrial automation, automobile control, and robotics, fuzzy logic can be utilized to represent and manage complicated systems.

### Hybrid Approach

This strategy uses a variety of AI methods to address challenging issues. In a hybrid method, for instance, data may be analyzed using machine learning to find patterns, and judgments may be made using logical reasoning to determine those patterns.

## 1.2.2 Types of Artificial Intelligence

1. **Narrow AI (Weak AI):** This type of AI is designed for more specific problem-solving within a limited domain.
    - It lacks general intelligence and is confined to its programmed purpose.
    - For example, AI-powered chess engines that can defeat grandmasters excel in one task but cannot perform beyond their predefined function.
2. **General AI (Strong AI):** Developing strong AI is significantly more complex than narrow AI.
    - It possesses human-like cognitive abilities, including reasoning, experiential learning, and decision-making.
3. **Super AI:** According to AI theorist Nick Bostrom, A super-intelligent system can outperform human capabilities exponentially, potentially exceeding human intelligence by trillions of times.
    - This represents the highest level of AI advancement.

## AI Systems and Intelligent Agents

An AI system usually consists of many agent and its environment. An agent is any entity, such as a robot or human, capable of perceiving its surroundings through sensors and acting using effectors.

In traditional planning, the agent assumes that it is the only system affecting the world, ensuring predictable outcomes.

However, in dynamic environments with multiple actors, an agent must assess uncertainty, refine predictions, and adapt based on observations.

### Key AI Technologies

- **Machine Learning:** Without explicit programming, machines can learn from data and generate predictions thanks to algorithms.
- **Natural Language Processing (NLP):** Enables machines to comprehend, analyze, and generate human language.
- **Computer Vision:** AI models process and interpret visual data from images and videos.
- **Robotics:** AI-powered automation systems assist in various fields, including manufacturing, healthcare, and logistics.

- **Neural Networks:** Inspired by the human brain, these models enhance pattern recognition and deep learning capabilities.
- **Expert Systems:** AI-driven programs replicate human decision-making in specific domains.
- **Chatbots:** Virtual assistants powered by AI that interact with users via text or voice.

### Challenges in Artificial Intelligence

Despite its advancements, AI presents several challenges:

- **Bias & Fairness:** AI models may inherit and amplify biases from data, leading to unfair outcomes.
- **Transparency Issues:** Complex AI decision-making processes can be difficult to interpret, making accountability challenging.
- **Job Automation:** AI may replace human jobs, necessitating workforce reskilling.
- **Privacy & Security:** AI systems collect and analyze vast personal data, posing privacy risks and cybersecurity threats.
- **Ethical Considerations:** AI raises concerns related to autonomy, accountability, and moral decision-making.
- **Regulation Needs:** Proper policies are essential to ensure AI development and deployment align with ethical and societal norms.
- Future AI Trends
- **Reinforcement Learning:** A technique where AI agents learn through interactions with their environment.
- **Explainable AI:** Focuses on improving AI model transparency and interpretability.
- **Generative AI:** Creates new, realistic content by recognizing underlying data patterns.
- **Quantum AI:** Combines AI with quantum computing to solve complex problems beyond classical computing capabilities.
- This rephrased version presents the same concepts but in a fresh and original manner. Let me know if you'd like any refinements!

## 1.3 AGENTS IN ARTIFICIAL INTELLIGENCE

In artificial intelligence (AI), the study of rational agents and their interactions with the environment plays a crucial role. Agents rely on sensors to perceive their surroundings and actuators to respond accordingly. These AI agents can possess various cognitive attributes, such as knowledge, beliefs, and objectives. An agent is any entity capable of sensing its environment and taking action based on that information. This process follows a continuous cycle of perception, reasoning, and execution. There are different types of agents, including human agents, where sensory organs like eyes and ears act as sensors, while hands, legs, and vocal tracts serve as actuators. Robotic agents use cameras, infrared sensors, and natural language processing systems to gather data, while motors and mechanical components act as actuators. Similarly, software agents process digital inputs, such as keystrokes or file data, and produce outputs on a screen. Essentially, everything around us, from smartphones to thermostats and cameras, can function as an agent. To understand agents better, it is essential to recognize the role of sensors, effectors, and actuators. A sensor detects environmental changes and transmits data to electronic systems, enabling perception. Actuators convert energy into motion, allowing machines to perform tasks, including motors, gears, and mechanical components. Effectors are devices that enable interaction with the environment, such as wheels, limbs, display screens, or robotic arms. Collectively, these elements empower AI agents to function efficiently across various applications.

An autonomous entity that uses sensors and actuators to interact with its surroundings in order to accomplish particular objectives is known as an intelligent agent. These agents can learn from their surroundings to improve their decision-making process. A common example of an intelligent agent is a thermostat, which adjusts temperature based on environmental conditions. The functioning of AI agents is governed by four fundamental principles: they must be capable of perceiving their environment, making decisions based on observations, executing actions following those decisions, and acting rationally in all situations. A rational agent operates with a clear preference, accounts for uncertainty, and optimizes its actions to maximize performance. In AI, rational agents are essential for applications in game theory and decision-making, ensuring that they make the most effective choices in various real-world scenarios. The concept of rationality is particularly crucial in reinforcement learning algorithms, where agents receive positive rewards for optimal actions and negative rewards for incorrect ones. While intelligent and rational agents share many similarities, their distinction lies in decision-making strategies. Rationality is evaluated based on factors such as performance metrics, prior knowledge of the environment, the best possible actions available, and the sequence of perceptions. However, rationality should not be confused with omniscience, as omniscient agents operate with complete knowledge of all possible outcomes, which is unrealistic in practical applications.

## 1.4 STRUCTURE OF AN AI AGENT

Knowledge of architecture and agent programs is necessary to comprehend the structure of intelligent agents. The equipment on which the agent operates is called the architecture. It is a gadget that has sensors and actuators, like a computer, a camera, and a robotic automobile. An implementation of an agent function is called an agent program. There are numerous instances of artificial intelligence agents. Messages, reminders, and appointment scheduling are just a few of the duties that intelligent personal assistants are meant to aid users with. Siri, Alexa, and Google Assistant are a few instances of personal assistants.

- **Autonomous robots:** These are agents made to function independently in the real environment. They are capable of carrying out duties including sorting, cleaning, and product delivery. The Roomba vacuum and the Amazon delivery robot are two instances of autonomous robots.
- Agents made specifically to play games, either against other agents or human opponents, are known as gaming agents. Agents that play poker and chess are two examples of gaming agents.
- **Fraud detection agents:** These are agents created to identify instances of financial transaction fraud. They are able to spot suspect conduct and notify authorities by analyzing patterns of behavior. Banks and credit card firms are two examples of fraud detection agents.
- **Traffic management agents:** These are agents made specifically to control the flow of traffic in urban areas. To reduce congestion, they can divert cars, modify

traffic lights, and keep an eye on traffic trends. Agents deployed in smart cities worldwide are examples of traffic management.

- Keystrokes, file contents, files, transmitted network packets that function as actuators, and received network packages that serve as sensors and screen displays are all part of a software agent.
- The hands, legs, mouth, and other bodily parts of a human agent function as actuators, while the eyes, ears, and other organs serve as sensors.
- Various motors function as actuators, and cameras and infrared rangefinders serve as sensors in a robotic agent.

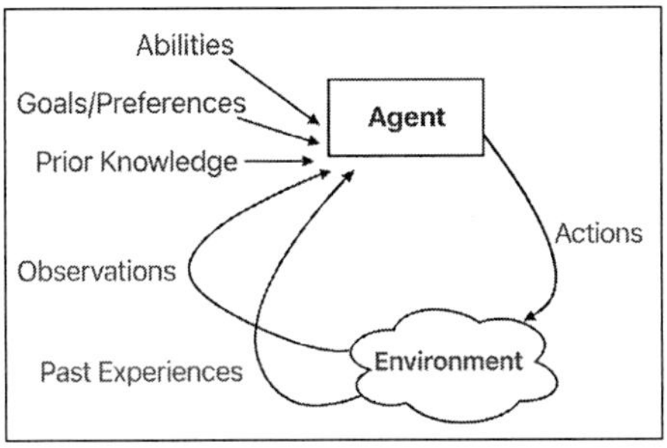


***Figure 1.1:*** *Characteristics of an Agent*

## 1.5 TYPES OF AGENTS

Agents can be grouped into five classes based on their degree of perceived intelligence and capability:

- Model-Based Reflex Agents
- Goal-Based Agents
- Utility-Based Agents
- Learning Agent
- Multi-agent systems
- Hierarchical agents Simple Reflex Agents

### 1.5.1 Simple Reflex Agents

Simple reflex agents operate purely based on their current perception, ignoring past experiences or percept history. An agent's percept history is essentially a record of everything it has observed up to that point. These agents function by following a condition-action rule, where specific actions are triggered by particular conditions. If the condition is satisfied, the action is executed; otherwise, it is not. This approach is effective in environments that are fully observable, but in partially observable settings, simple reflex agents often fall into infinite loops. One way to prevent this is by introducing randomness into the agent's behavior, allowing it to break free from repetitive cycles.

- Despite their simplicity, reflex agents have several limitations:
- They have minimal intelligence and cannot learn from past experiences.
- They lack awareness of non-perceptual aspects of the environment.
- The ruleset can become excessively large, making storage and retrieval difficult.

If the environment changes, the rules must be modified accordingly, making them inflexible.

While simple reflex agents work well in straightforward, predictable environments, they struggle with complexity and adaptability.

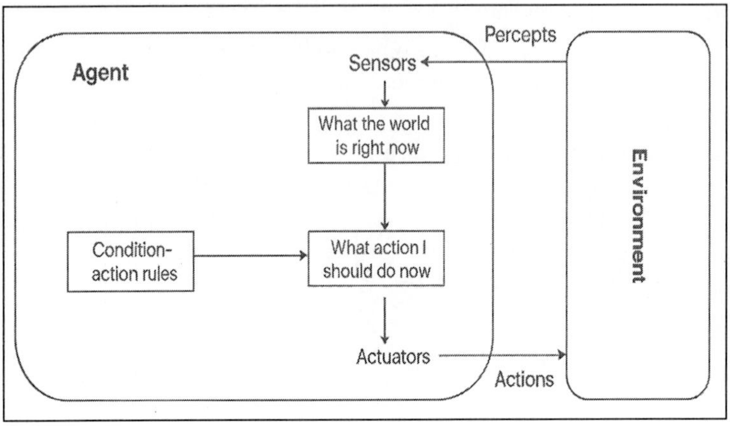


***Figure 1.2:*** *Simple Reflex Agents*

## 1.5.2 Model-Based Reflex Agents

A model-based agent functions by recognizing a rule that aligns with the current situation. In contrast to basic reflex agents, it can manage partially visible surroundings by sustaining an internal representation of the world.

This model allows the agent to track information beyond what is immediately perceptible. The agent continuously updates its internal state based on its percept history, modifying it with each new observation. By storing and structuring information about the unseen aspects of the environment, the agent can make more informed decisions.

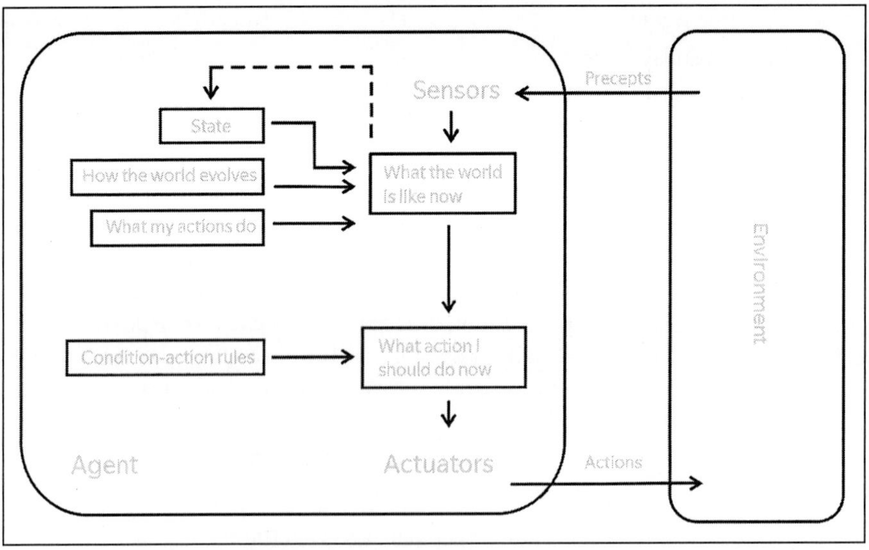


***Figure 1.3:*** *Model-Based Reflex Agents*

To update its internal state effectively, the agent must understand how the world changes independently and how its own actions influence the external environment. This enables it to predict future states and adapt accordingly, making it more flexible and capable than simple reflex agents.

### 1.5.3 Goal-Based Agents

Goal-based agents make decisions by evaluating their proximity to a desired outcome or target state. Each activity they undertake is aimed at advancing them toward their objective.

By assessing different possibilities, the agent selects the most effective path toward the desired state. These agents are highly adaptable since the criteria guiding their choices are clearly defined and can be adjusted as needed. Typically, they rely on planning and search algorithms to determine the best course of action. One of their key advantages is that their behavior can be easily modified based on new goals or changing circumstances.

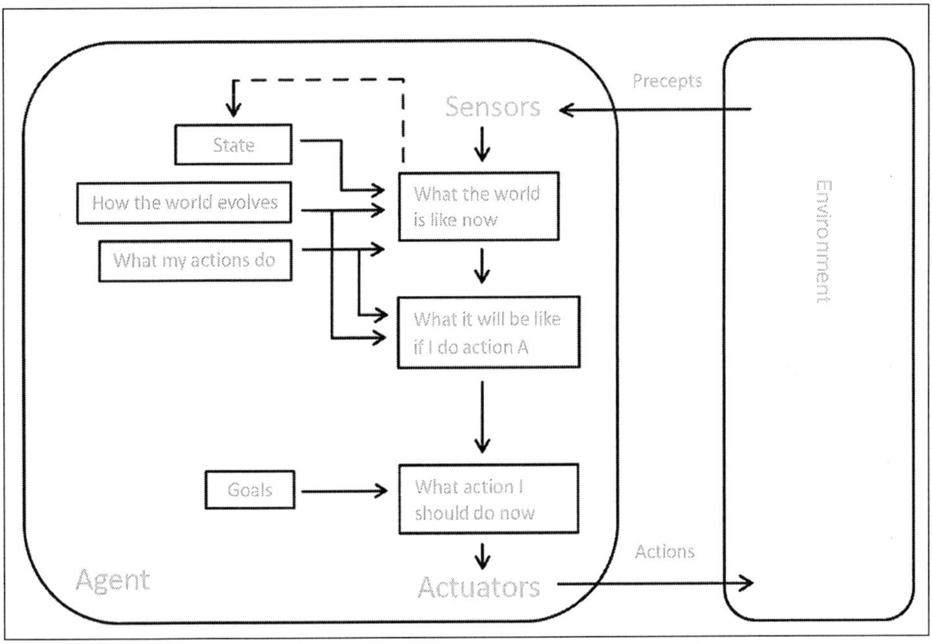


***Figure 1.4:*** *Goal-Based Agents*

### 1.5.4 Utility-Based Agents

Utility-based agents are designed with their end applications in mind, allowing them to evaluate multiple options and determine the best course of action. When faced with several choices, these agents make decisions based on a utility function, which assigns a preference or value to each possible state. Simply achieving a goal may not always be enough—factors like speed, safety, and cost may also be important. Utility measures an agent's level of satisfaction, ensuring that it selects the action that maximizes expected utility, especially in uncertain environments. The utility function helps quantify satisfaction by mapping different states to numerical values, allowing the agent to make more informed and optimal decisions.

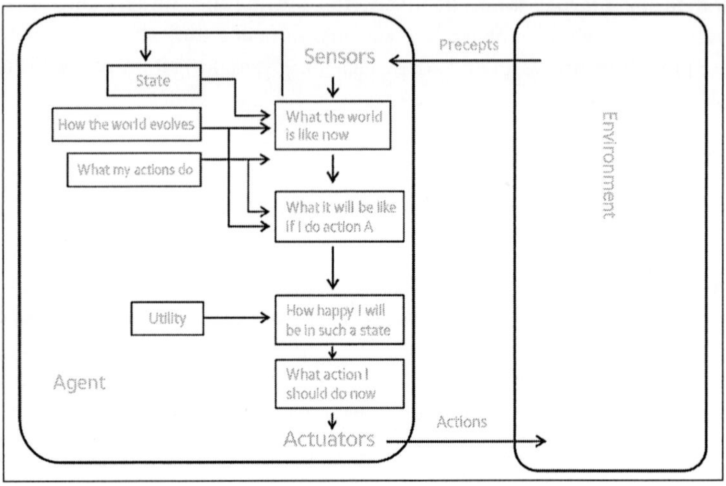


*Figure 1.5: Utility-Based Agents*

## 1.5.5 Learning Agent

A learning agent in artificial intelligence (AI) has the ability to improve its performance based on past experiences. Initially, it operates using predefined knowledge but gradually learns to adapt and make independent decisions. It consists of four key components:

1. **Learning Element :** Responsible for enhancing the agent's capabilities by acquiring knowledge from its environment.
2. **Critic :** Evaluates the agent's performance by comparing it against a set benchmark and providing feedback.
3. **Performance Element :** Determines and executes actions based on the acquired knowledge.
4. **Problem Generator :** Suggests new actions to encourage exploration and gain valuable learning experiences.

These components work together to help the agent evolve and improve over time.

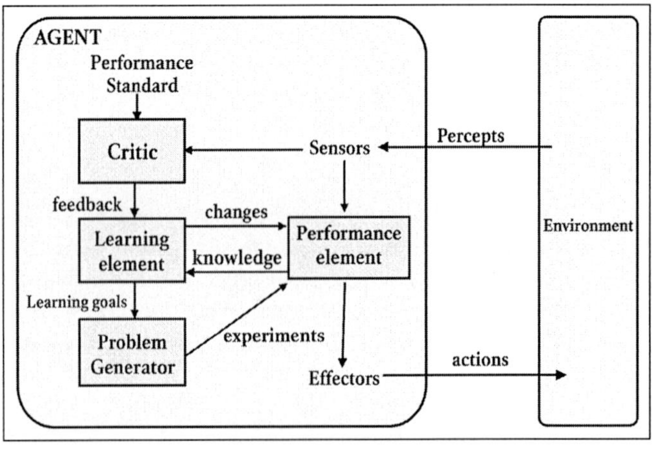


*Figure 1.6: Learning Agent*

### 1.5.6 Multi-Agent Systems

To accomplish a shared objective, these agents communicate with one another. To accomplish their goal, they might need to coordinate their efforts and speak with one another. A system made up of several interacting agents intended to cooperate in order to accomplish a shared objective is known as a multi-agent system (MAS). These agents can perceive their surroundings, make judgments, and act to accomplish the shared goal. They can be either fully or partially autonomous. Applications for MAS are numerous and include social networks, robotics, and transportation systems. In complex systems, they can contribute to increased flexibility, cost savings, and efficiency.

A number of features, including whether the agents are homogeneous or heterogeneous, cooperative or competitive, and have similar or distinct goals, can be used to categorize MAS into several categories. Coordination may become more difficult as a result, although systems may become more durable and versatile.

In cooperative MAS, agents collaborate to accomplish a shared objective, whereas in competitive MAS, agents compete with one another to accomplish their individual objectives. In certain situations, MAS may also require agents to balance their own goals with the group's interests, involving both cooperative and competitive behavior. A variety of methods, including machine learning, game theory, and agent-based modeling, can be used to implement MAS. Agents' strategic interactions are analyzed and their behavior is predicted using game theory. Agents are trained using machine learning to gradually enhance their decision-making skills. Simulating complex systems and researching agent interactions are two applications of agent-based modeling. All things considered, multi-agent systems are an effective artificial intelligence tool that can assist in resolving challenging issues and boost productivity across a range of uses.

### 1.5.7 Hierarchical Agents

High-level agents supervise the actions of lower-level agents in this hierarchical organization. While the low-level agents do particular tasks, the high-level agents set objectives and limitations. In complicated environments with numerous tasks and subtasks, hierarchical agents are helpful.

Agents arranged in a hierarchy, where higher-level agents supervise the actions of lower-level agents, are known as hierarchical agents. While the low-level agents do particular tasks, the high-level agents set objectives and limitations. In complicated contexts, this framework enables more ordered and effective decision-making.

Several applications, such as robotics, manufacturing, and transportation systems, can use hierarchical agents. They are especially helpful in settings where a large number of activities and subtasks require prioritization and coordination.

In a hierarchical agent system, the higher-level agents are in charge of establishing the objectives and limitations for the agents at lower levels. Usually, the system's ultimate goal serves as the foundation for these objectives and limitations. For instance, in a manufacturing system, the high-level agents may use client demand to determine the production goals for the lower-level agents.

In order to accomplish the objectives established by the high-level agents, the low-level agents must complete certain tasks. Depending on the particular application, these activities could be rather easy or highly complicated. For instance, low-level agents may be in charge of controlling traffic flow at particular crossings in a transportation system.

Depending on the system's complexity, hierarchical agents can be arranged into several tiers. There might only be two tiers in a basic system: high-level agents and low-level agents. Multiple levels may exist in a more complicated system, with intermediate-level agents in charge of directing the actions of lower-level agents.

The ability to use resources more effectively is one benefit of hierarchical agents. It is feasible to assign tasks to the agents most qualified to complete them without causing duplication of effort by arranging agents in a hierarchy. Decision-making may become quicker and more effective as a result, and the system may function better overall. All things considered, hierarchical agents are an effective artificial intelligence tool that may be used to tackle challenging issues and boost productivity in a range of settings.

The ability to use resources more effectively is one benefit of hierarchical agents. It is feasible to assign tasks to the agents most qualified to complete them without causing duplication of effort by arranging agents in a hierarchy. Decision-making may become quicker and more effective as a result, and the system may function better overall. All things considered, hierarchical agents are an effective artificial intelligence tool that may be used to tackle challenging issues and boost productivity in a range of settings.

### 1.5.8 Applications for Agents

Artificial intelligence uses agents for a variety of purposes, such as:

- **Robotics:** In the transportation, manufacturing, and other sectors, agents can be employed to operate robots and automate activities.
- **Smart buildings and homes:** Agents can optimize energy use and enhance comfort by controlling lighting, heating, and other systems in smart buildings and houses.<br>**Transportation systems:** Agents can enhance supply chain management and logistics, optimize routes for self-driving cars, and control traffic flow.
- **Healthcare:** Agents can be used to maximize the use of healthcare resources, monitor patients, and create individualized treatment regimens.
- **Finance:** In the financial sector, agents can be employed for risk management, automated trading, and fraud detection.
- **Games:** Agents can be utilized to build clever opponents in simulations and games, giving players a more difficult and realistic experience.
- **Natural language processing:** Agents can be used to answer questions, translate languages, and create chatbots that can converse with users in natural language.
- **Cybersecurity:** Network security, malware analysis, and intrusion detection may all be done with agents.
- **Environmental monitoring:** Agents can be utilized to assess climate change, oversee natural resources, and improve environmental sustainability.
- **Social media:** Agents may analyze data from social media, identify trends and patterns, and provide consumers with personalized suggestions. Ultimately, agents represent a proficient and versatile artificial intelligence instrument capable of addressing diverse challenges across several domains.

## 1.6 PROBLEM-SOLVING AGENT IN ARTIFICIAL INTELLIGENCE

Artificial intelligence problem-solving can be highly intricate, involving the utilization of numerous methods and data structures. The Problem-Solving Agent, which assists machines in solving problems, is one important participant. What is an agent that solves problems? There are numerous kinds of difficulties that can be resolved, and the approaches taken will vary depending on the particular issue. Solving a maze or navigation puzzle is the most prevalent kind of challenge. Finding solutions to systems of equations, forecasting results, and seeing patterns are examples of other problem kinds. Every kind of problem can be solved using a different collection of methods and resources.

Artificial intelligence problem-solving involves three primary steps:

(1) **Understanding the problem:** This step entails comprehending the problem's particulars and determining the necessary course of action.

(2) **Creating potential solutions:** This stage entails producing as many potential solutions as you can using the problem's details and your understanding of computer operation.

(3) **Selecting a solution:** This phase entails determining the best choice given your knowledge of the issue and your available options.

## Types of Agents

That Solve Problems An artificial intelligence subset known as "problem-solving agents" aids in automating the process of solving problems. Natural language, algebra, calculus, statistics, and machine learning problems can all be resolved with them. Automata, predicate, and propositional agents are the three categories of problem-solving agents. Propositional problem-solving agents are able to comprehend basic instructions such as "find the maximum value of x" or "draw a line between A and B." Predicate problem-solving agents are able to comprehend more complicated phrases such as "find all pairs of snakes in a jar" or "find the shortest path between two points." Automata, the most basic type of problem-solving agent, are limited to comprehending symbol sequences, such as "draw a square."

## Categorization of Problems Solving Agents

General problem solvers and domain-specific issue solvers are two categories of problem-solving agents. Domain-specific issue solvers are more suited to handling particular kinds of problems, whereas general problem solvers can answer a broad variety of problems. AI systems that are made to address general artificial intelligence (AI) issues, such figuring out how to play games or navigate a 3D world, are known as general problem solvers. Programs designed to address particular problem types, like photo editing or medical diagnostics, are known as domain-specific problem solvers. Both general and domain-specific problem-solving agents can be used in conjunction with other AI tools, including natural language processing (NLP) algorithms and machine learning models.

## Problem-Solving Agent Applications

There are several applications for problem-solving agents in artificial intelligence. They can be applied to generalize an issue and provide possible solutions, or they can be utilized to assist in solving particular tasks or difficulties. Either way, the problem-solving agent can comprehend intricate instructions and complete certain tasks.

## 1.7 UNINFORMED AND INFORMED SEARCH STRATEGIES

### Informed and Uninformed Search in AI

In artificial intelligence, an informed search utilizes additional knowledge about the goal state to enhance search efficiency. This is achieved through a function that estimates a state's closeness to the desired outcome, allowing the algorithm to navigate more effectively. Unlike uninformed search algorithms, informed search methods use supplementary data such as heuristics and cost estimates to prioritize which paths to explore, making problem-solving more efficient.

- **Heuristic Utilization:** They employ heuristics to guide the search process, determining which nodes should be expanded next.
- **Efficiency:** By eliminating unpromising paths, they outperform uninformed methods like Breadth-First Search (BFS) or Depth-First Search (DFS).
- **Goal-Directed Approach:** Their primary focus is solving a specific problem efficiently.
- **Cost-Based Evaluation:** They assess nodes based on cost estimations, considering the path cost or projected cost to reach the goal.
- **Prioritization:** They rank nodes based on newly acquired information, improving decision-making.
- **Optimality:** If the heuristics used are admissible (never overestimate the actual cost) and consistent (provide a lower bound on the cost), informed search algorithms can guarantee optimal solutions.

On the other hand, an uninformed search operates without additional knowledge about the goal state beyond what is explicitly defined in the problem statement. These algorithms explore the search space blindly, without considering the cost of reaching the solution or the likelihood of finding an optimal path.

Common examples include Breadth-First Search (BFS), Depth-First Search (DFS), and Depth-Limited Search. Uninformed searches are often used for basic problem exploration or as a foundation for more advanced search techniques. However, in complex problems with vast search spaces, they can become highly inefficient due to the exponential growth of explored states.

Key characteristics of uninformed search algorithms include:

- **Systematic Exploration:** These algorithms expand nodes in a structured manner, either level-wise (BFS) or depth-wise until a limit is reached (DFS).
- **Absence of Heuristics:** Unlike informed search, they do not rely on extra information such as cost estimates.
- **Blind Searching:** They do not consider the probability of finding a solution quickly or the cost of achieving the goal.
- **Simplicity:** These methods are easy to implement and understand, making them useful for foundational algorithm development.

While uninformed search methods provide a fundamental approach to problem-solving, informed search techniques offer greater efficiency and are preferred for complex AI applications.

## SUMMARY

Artificial Intelligence (AI) is the discipline focused on creating systems that can mimic human cognitive abilities such as learning, reasoning, and decision-making. It finds widespread application in areas like healthcare, finance, robotics, and customer service, proving its value through increased efficiency and automation. The foundations of AI lie in disciplines like computer science and mathematics, employing methods such as machine learning, neural networks, and logical reasoning. AI can be categorized into narrow, general, and super intelligence based on its capability. Central to AI is the concept of agents—entities that perceive their environment through sensors and act using actuators to achieve goals. These agents come in various types, including simple reflex, model-based, goal-based, utility-based, and learning agents, each with different levels of complexity. Problem-solving agents are a special class designed to tackle defined challenges by evaluating various strategies. To do this, they use search techniques, which are divided into uninformed (like breadth-first and depth-first search) that work without prior knowledge, and informed strategies (like A* and greedy search) that use heuristics to improve efficiency.

## CASE STUDY

A hospital has implemented an AI-powered diagnostic system to assist doctors in detecting diseases such as cancer, pneumonia, and cardiovascular conditions. The system employs deep learning algorithms that have been trained on extensive patient data, medical imaging, and historical diagnoses.

Over time, the hospital has observed improved diagnostic accuracy and faster patient evaluations. However, some challenges have emerged, including ethical concerns about AI decision-making, data privacy issues, and the need for human oversight.

### Discussion Questions

1. How can AI improve the accuracy and efficiency of medical diagnosis?
2. What ethical concerns arise from using AI in healthcare decision-making?
3. How can hospitals balance AI automation with the need for human expertise?
4. What measures should be taken to ensure patient data privacy and security in AI-driven healthcare systems?
5. How can AI be further improved to enhance its effectiveness in the medical field?

# Artificial Neural Networks

2

UNIT

## 2.1 ARTIFICIAL NEURAL NETWORK: AN OVERVIEW

A mathematical framework known as an artificial neural network (ANN) is modelled after the composition and operations of biological neural networks, which are present in the human brain. The term originates from biological neurons, which are interconnected to process and transmit information. Similarly, in an ANN, artificial neurons—often referred to as nodes or units—are interconnected in multiple layers to perform tasks such as pattern recognition, decision-making, and predictive analysis. These networks consist of three primary layers: The input layer is where initial information or inputs are received. Hidden Layers: Utilize activation functions as well as weighted connections to process data; The output layer generates the final outcome or forecast.

ANNs are extensively utilized in machine learning applications such as prediction of finances, recognition of images, speech recognition, as well as healthcare diagnosis. Their ability to learn patterns and improve performance over time makes them a powerful tool in artificial intelligence.

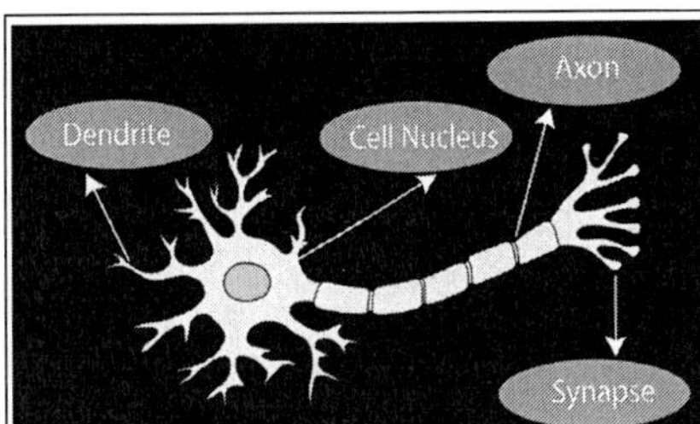


**Figure 2.1:** *Biological Neural Network*

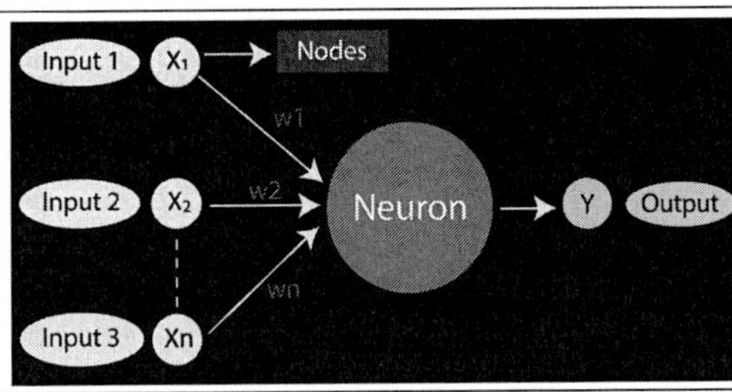


**Figure 2.2:** *Artificial Neural Network*

### 2.1.1 Comparison Between Biological & Artificial Neurons

ANNs are inspired by the biological neurons found in animal brains, sharing similarities in both structure and function.

Signals are received by biological neurons' dendrites, analyzed by the cell body (soma), and then sent to other neurons via axons. Analogously, in ANN, information is received by input nodes, processed by hidden layers, and then used by output layers to produce the final result using activation functions.

The synapses in biological neurons serve as connections that allow impulses to travel from dendrites to the soma. In ANNs, this function is represented by weights, which analyses the connection strength in-between nodes. Knowledge in biological neurons occurs in the soma, where impulses that exceed a threshold trigger an action potential, enabling information transmission. This process is influenced by synaptic plasticity, which allows synapses to change their strength based on experience. In artificial neural networks, learning happens through backpropagation, an algorithm that adjusts node weights by minimizing the error between predicted and actual outputs.

Additionally, activation in biological neurons occurs when impulses surpass a threshold, prompting them to fire. In ANNs, this process is replicated through activation functions, which apply mathematical transformations to input data to produce an output.

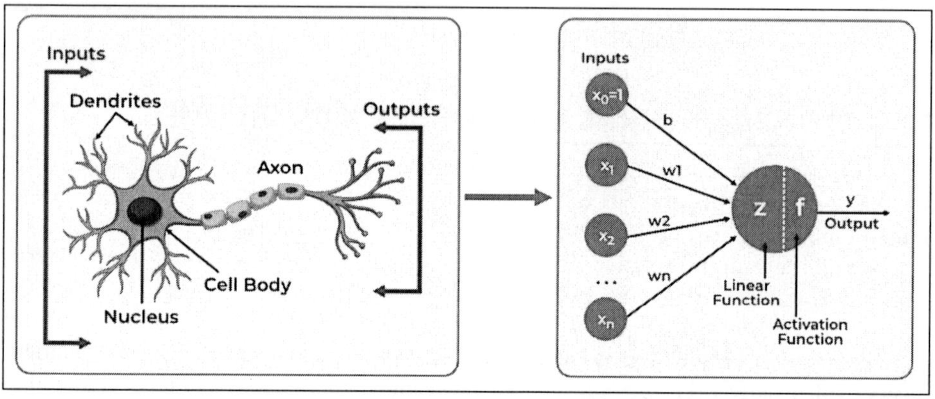


***Figure 2.3:*** *Biological neurons to Artificial neurons*

To verify the ANN's accuracy, human feedback is used to confirm whether the network's predictions are correct. If the ANN misidentifies an image, a technique called backpropagation is applied to adjust the model. This process involves modifying the connection weights in the ANN based on the error rate, ensuring the network improves over time. Training continues until the ANN can correctly classify cat images with minimal errors.

## 2.2 STRUCTURE OF ANN

Investigating the structure of neural networks is crucial to comprehending how they work. Several artificial neurons, often referred to as units, arranged into various layers make up an ANN. Together, these layers process data and generate precise forecasts.

The three main layers of an artificial neural network are as follows:

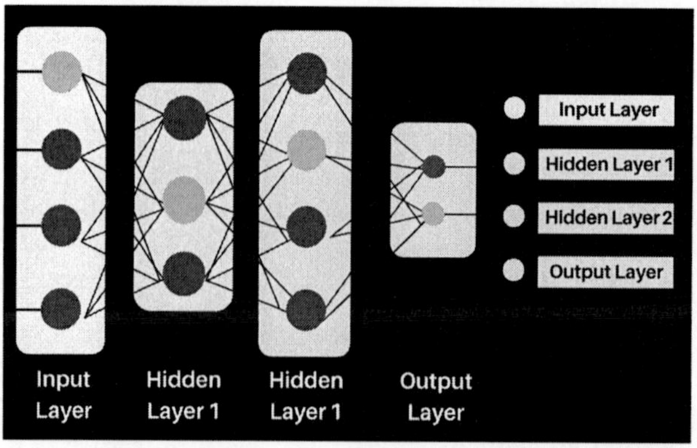


***Figure 2.4:*** *The Structure and Functioning of Artificial Neural Networks*

## Network Layers in Artificial Neural Networks

- **Input Layer:** As the name suggests, this layer receives data from the external environment or a programmer in different formats.
- **Hidden Layer:** Positioned between the I/O layers, this layer achieves all the necessary computations to identify hidden patterns as well as features within the data.
- **Output Layer:** After undergoing several transformations in the hidden layer, the processed data reaches the output layer, which presents the final result.

An ANN incorporates a bias term and computes the weighted sum of inputs. A transfer function is used to express this computation. The activation function then determines whether a node should be activated, allowing only certain signals to progress to the output layer. Different activation functions are available, depending on the nature of the task.

## Applications of ANNs

- **Parallel Processing Capability:** ANNs can process multiple tasks simultaneously due to their ability to handle computations in parallel.
- **Distributed Data Storage:** Unlike traditional programming, where data is stored in a centralized database, ANNs distribute data across the entire network. Even if some portions of the network are lost, it can still function effectively.
- **Handling Incomplete Data:** Even when provided with insufficient data, a trained ANN can still produce useful outputs. The accuracy of the results depends on how significant the missing data is.
- **Adaptive Learning:** ANNs can adjust and improve their performance by learning from examples. However, if a network is not exposed to a full range of scenarios, it may generate inaccurate outputs.
- **Fault Tolerance:** If certain neurons or network components become faulty, ANNs can still function, demonstrating a level of resilience in their computations.

## Limitations of Artificial Neural Networks

- **Defining the Right Network Architecture:** There is no fixed rule for designing the optimal ANN structure. It is often determined through trial and error, requiring expertise and experience.
- **Lack of Explainability:** One of the biggest challenges with ANNs is their black-box nature—they generate solutions without explaining how or why a particular result was obtained, reducing their transparency.
- **Hardware Dependence:** Due to their design, ANNs require specialized hardware with parallel processing capabilities, making them reliant on advanced computational resources.
- **Preprocessing Data for ANN:** Prior to being fed to the network, problems must be transformed into numerical values because ANNs are generally used to handle numerical input. The way data is presented significantly impacts network performance, requiring careful consideration by the user.

## How Do Artificial Neural Networks Function?

The ANN receives input signals from external sources in the form of vector images or patterns. These inputs are mathematically expressed using x(n) notation, where n represents the number of input values. The network processes these inputs through multiple layers, adjusting connection weights and biases to refine predictions and improve accuracy over time.

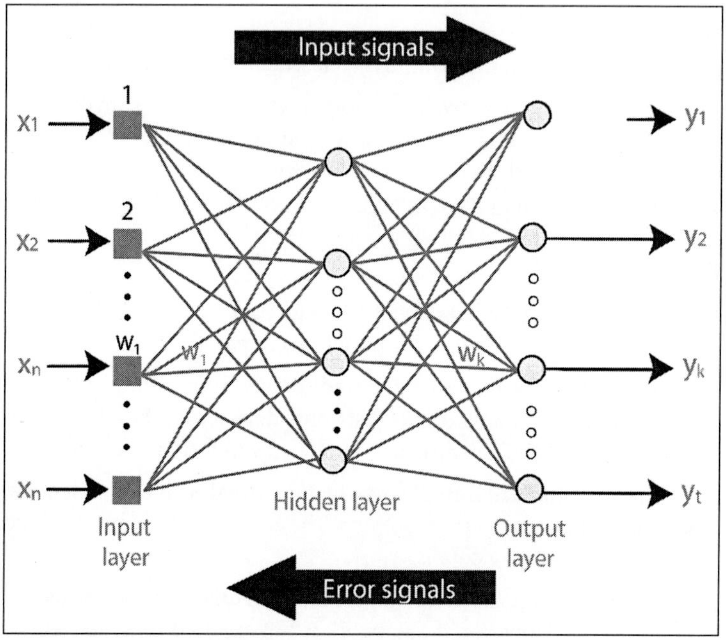


***Figure 2.5:*** *Structure of ANN*

The input values are first multiplied by their corresponding weights, which play a crucial role in enabling artificial neural networks to address specific problems. These weights often dictate how strongly neurons in the network are connected to one another. All of the weighted inputs are then added together by the computing unit. When the weighted total equals zero, a bias term is added to either prevent the output from becoming zero or to modify the system's reaction. In this case, the bias shares the same input and the weight is set to 1. The weighted inputs' sum can therefore be anywhere between zero and positive infinity. An activation function is added to the total of the weighted inputs, and a predetermined maximum value is utilized as a reference to maintain the result within the intended range.

A collection of transfer functions called the activation function aids in achieving the desired result. These functions can be broadly classified as linear or non-linear. Common activation functions include binary, linear, and hyperbolic tangent (TanH) sigmoidal functions. Let's explore each one:

## Binary Activation Function

This function produces an output of either 0 or 1 based on a threshold value. If the total weighted input surpasses the threshold, the output is 1; otherwise, it remains 0.

Among ANN, one of the most fundamental network is feedforward neural network. The input, or data, in this ANN only moves in one direction. The input layer is where it enters the ANN, and the output layer is where it leaves, with hidden layers perhaps present or absent.

Therefore, the feedforward neural network typically lacks backpropagation and simply has a front-propagated wave. There are various weights attached to the connection. Since there isn't a feedback loop, the signal can only go from input to output. It can be separated into the two categories listed below. – A feedforward network with a single layer The idea is a feedforward artificial neural network with a single weighted layer. To put it another way, the input layer and the output layer are completely interconnected.

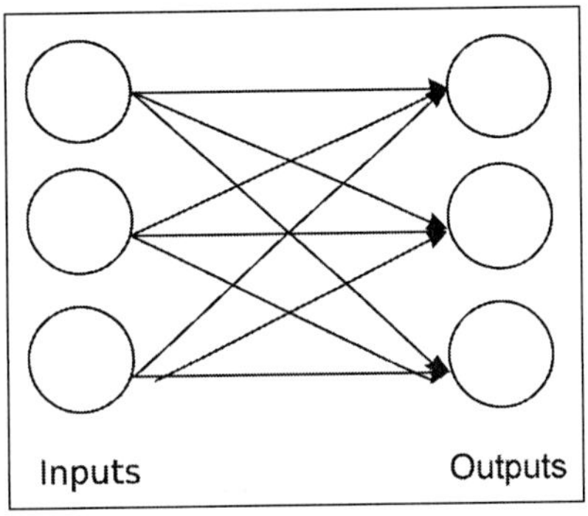


***Figure 2.6:*** *Single layer Feedforward neural network*

The idea behind a multilayer feedforward network is that feedforward artificial neural networks (ANNs) include many weighted layers. Due to the presence of a few layers between the input as well as output layers, these networks are referred to as hidden layers.

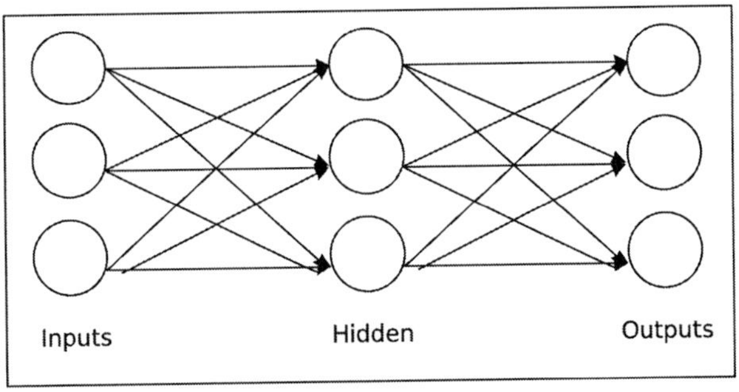


***Figure 2.7:*** *Multi-Layer Feedforward neural network*

A feedback network, includes pathways that allow signals to pass as loops, moving in forward as well as backward directions. This characteristic makes it a non-linear dynamic system that continuously updates until it reaches a stable state. Feedback networks can be classified into different types, including recurrent networks.

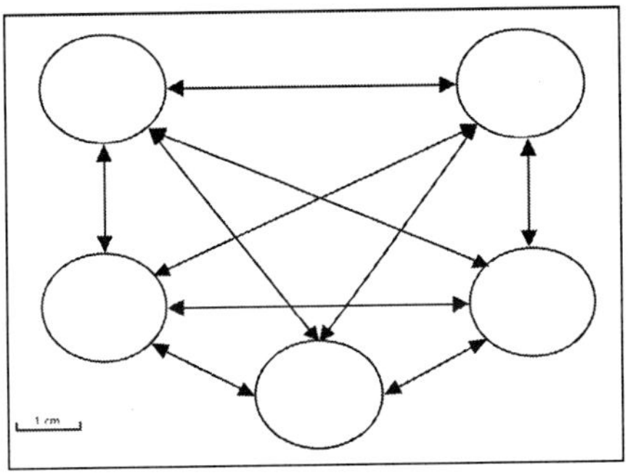

***Figure 2.8:*** *Feedback Network*

Jordan network – A Jordan network is a type of closed-loop network where the output is fed back into the system as an input, creating a continuous feedback cycle. This feedback mechanism allows the network to retain information from previous states, enhancing its ability to process sequential data.

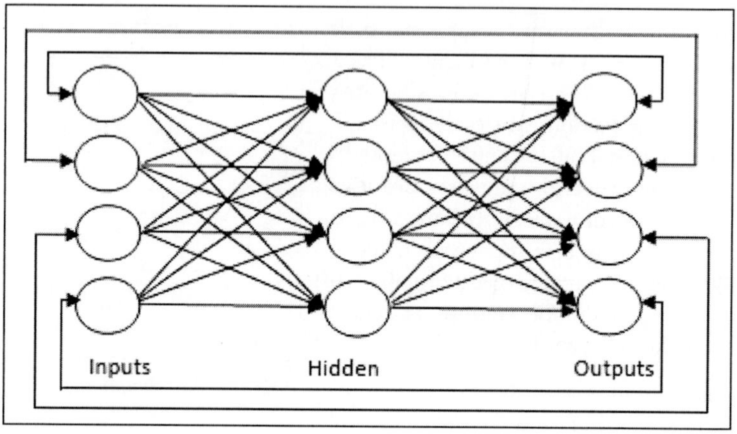


***Figure 2.9:*** *Jordan network*

## Convolutional Neural Network

A Convolutional Neural Network (CNN) include one or more convolutional layers that process input data by applying convolution operations before passing the results to subsequent layers. These networks are widely used in image and audio processing, making them particularly useful for applications in computer vision.

A modular neural network consists of multiple independent neural networks that work separately to achieve a common goal without interacting with each other. Unlike traditional neural networks, each module is responsible for a specific sub-task and processes unique inputs. The main advantage of modular neural networks is their capacity to simplify difficult computational tasks by dividing them into smaller, manageable components while still producing accurate results.

Radial Basis Function (RBF) networks use a mathematical function that considers a point's distance from a central reference point. These networks typically have two layers: the Initial (first) layer synchronizes the input data with radial basis functions in the hidden layer, while the next (second) layer computes the final output. RBF networks are particularly effective for modeling data patterns and trends.

A Recurrent Neural Network (RNN) improves predictions by storing outputs from previous layers and feeding them back as input. The first layer of an RNN resembles a feed-forward neural network, but once the initial output is generated, the network begins utilizing feedback loops. Each unit in the network retains information from previous steps, allowing it to function as a memory cell and process sequential data effectively.

## Applications of ANN

- **Social Media:** ANN play a significant role in social media platforms. For example, Facebook's "People You May Know" feature uses neural networks to analyze user interests, profiles, and friend connections to suggest potential friends. Another common application is facial recognition, where convolutional neural networks compare a person's facial features with stored data to identify matches.

- **Marketing and Sales:** E-commerce platforms like Amazon and Flipkart leverage neural networks to make product recommendations.Similarly, food delivery apps such as Zomato and Swiggy suggest restaurants based on users' preferences and order history. This technique, known as personalized marketing, is widely used across industries such as online book retailers, movie streaming services, and hospitality websites. Artificial neural networks help businesses tailor marketing efforts to individual customers, improving engagement and sales.
- **Healthcare:** Neural networks are revolutionizing healthcare by aiding in early disease detection. For instance, in oncology, AI-driven models can analyze microscopic images to identify malignant tissues with an accuracy comparable to experienced medical professionals. Additionally, facial analysis of patient images can help detect rare genetic disorders at an early stage. The use of neural networks in healthcare enhances diagnostic accuracy and improves the overall quality of medical treatment worldwide.
- **Virtual Assistants:** Popular voice assistants like Siri, Alexa, and Cortana utilize artificial neural networks and Natural Language Processing (NLP) for comprehending and reacting to human speech

These virtual assistants analyze voice commands, interpret meaning, and provide relevant responses, making them an integral part of modern technology.

## 2.3 SINGLE LAYER PERCEPTRON

A single processing unit in any neural network is called a perceptron. A basic neuron that divides its input into one or two categories was first presented by Frank Rosenblatt in 1958. A linear classifier used in supervised learning is the perceptron. It facilitates the organization of the input data.

A neural network unit called a perceptron performs an exact calculation to identify features in the input data. The primary function of a perceptron is to divide data into two categories.

The input is mapped between the necessary values, such as (0, 1) or (-1, 1), using the activation function. This is how a typical neural network appears:

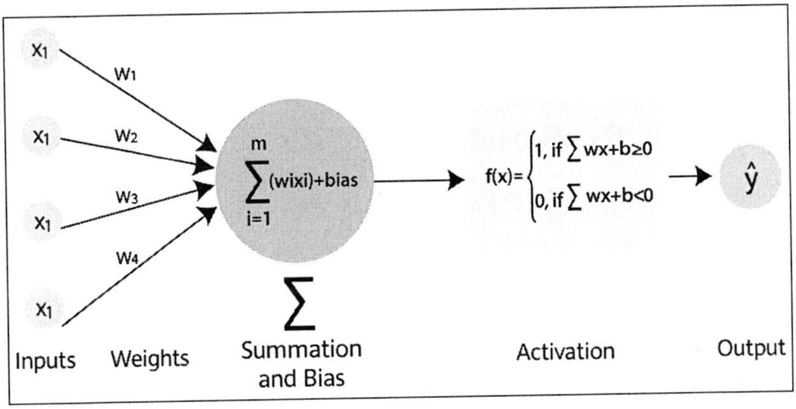


***Figure 2.10:*** *Single Layer Perceptron*

There are four components to the perceptron.

- **Enter a value or One layer of input:** Artificial input neurons comprise the perceptron' input layer, which receives and processes the initial data.
- **Bias and Weights:**
- **Weight:** This indicates the size or strength of the unit-to-unit connection.

### How Single Layer Perceptron Works?

A Single-Layer Perceptron (SLP) is the simplest form of an artificial neural network, primarily used for solving linearly separable problems. It consists of three main components: an input layer, a processing unit (or neuron), and an output layer. This model is based on the mathematical concept of a perceptron, introduced by Frank Rosenblatt in 1958, and serves as the foundation for more advanced neural networks.

### Working Mechanism of a Single-Layer Perceptron

1. **Receiving Input Data:** The perceptron takes multiple numerical inputs and assigns each a weight. The weights are crucial, as they influence how strongly an input contributes to the final decision.
2. **Summing Weighted Inputs:** It computes the sum of the inputs after multiplying each by its corresponding weight and adds a bias term.
3. **Adjusting Weights through Learning:** The perceptron undergoes training to adjust its weights based on errors in prediction. This is achieved through the Perceptron Learning Algorithm, which follows these steps:
    - Initialize weights and bias to small random values.
    - For each training example, compute the output.
    - Compare the output with the actual label.
    - Repeat this process until errors are minimized.

### Limitations of Single-Layer Perceptrons

- **Limited to Linearly Separable Problems:** A single-layer perceptron cannot handle problems where data is not linearly separable (e.g., XOR problem).
- **Lack of Hidden Layers:** It lacks additional processing layers, restricting its ability to capture complex relationships in data.
- **Simple Decision Boundaries:** The perceptron only learns straight-line decision boundaries, making it ineffective for more intricate classification tasks.

Despite its limitations, the single-layer perceptron remains a fundamental concept in artificial intelligence and neural networks, serving as a stepping stone for deeper learning architectures.

## 2.4 MULTI-LAYER PERCEPTRON

MLP is another term for multi-layer perception. Any input dimension can be converted to the desired dimension by its dense layers, which are entirely connected. A multi-layer neural network is known as a multi-layer perception. Neural networks are constructed by combining neurons in such a way that some of their outputs become inputs to other neurons.

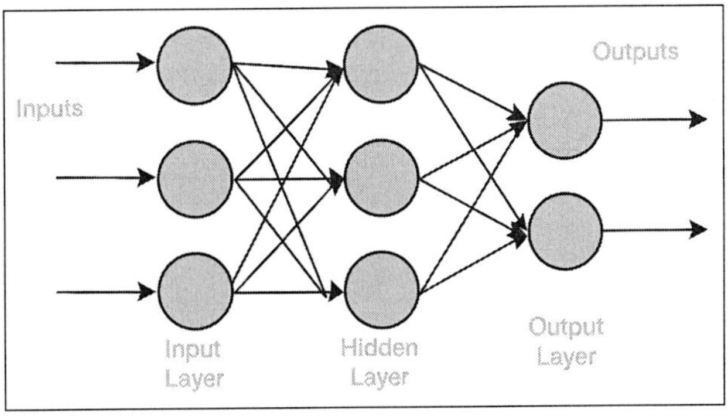


*Figure 2.11: Multi-layer Perceptron*

- An ANN kind called a Multilayer Perceptron (MLP) is made to process intricate patterns and correlations in data. Because of its numerous layers along with non-linear activation functions, an MLP can handle non-linear issues, unlike a Single-Layer Perceptron (SLP), which can only tackle straightforward, linearly distinguished problems.

## Structure of a Multilayer Perceptron

- The input layer acquires unprocessed data from an external source. Every neuron in the input layer represents a distinct aspect of the dataset.
- **Hidden Layers:** These intermediary layers process the information by applying weights, biases, and activation functions to identify intricate patterns. The more hidden layers present, the deeper the network, enhancing its ability to learn complex representations.
- **Output Layer:** The final layer generates predictions. The number of neurons in this layer depending on the nature of the task—one neuron for binary classification, while multiple neurons handle multi-class classification problems.

## Advantages of Multilayer Perceptrons

- **Handles Non-Linear Data:** MLPs can solve complex problems that simple perceptrons cannot.
- **Feature Extraction:** Automatically learns useful patterns from raw input, reducing manual preprocessing.
- **Universal Approximation:** With enough hidden layers and neurons, MLPs can approximate any continuous function.

## Limitations of Multilayer Perceptrons

- **Computationally Expensive:** Training deep networks requires high processing power.
- **Risk of Overfitting:** Complex models might memorize training data instead of generalizing well to new inputs.
- **Hyperparameter Sensitivity:** The choice of learning rate, number of layers, and activation functions must be fine-tuned for optimal performance.

- Despite these challenges, MLPs remain widely used in image recognition, speech processing, medical diagnosis, financial forecasting, and various AI applications, making them a crucial component in deep learning.

## 2.5 SUPERVISED AND UNSUPERVISED LEARNING

The two main categories of machine learning are supervised learning and unsupervised learning. This is determined by the type of training data and the algorithm's method for identifying patterns.

### Supervised learning

In machine learning, supervised learning is a technique where an algorithm is trained with labeled data, in which each input is associated with a known, accurate result. When faced with new, unseen data, the system can make precise predictions since it has discovered patterns and relationships through the analysis of these matched samples. This methodology is extensively employed in a number of domains, such as object detection, regression, and classification.

In supervised learning, the algorithm follows a structured learning process, continuously adjusting its internal parameters to reduce the gap between its predictions and the actual results. This refinement occurs through multiple training iterations, enabling the model to improve its accuracy over time. The ultimate objective is to build a system that can generalize well, meaning it can make reliable predictions even when working with unfamiliar data. Due to its ability to learn from historical examples, supervised learning is an essential tool in artificial intelligence applications, from spam detection in emails to medical diagnosis and financial forecasting.

For example, in an image classification task, a dataset might contain pictures of animals labeled as "Elephant," "Camel," or "Cow." The model analyzes these labeled images and learns to classify new images based on the patterns it has identified.

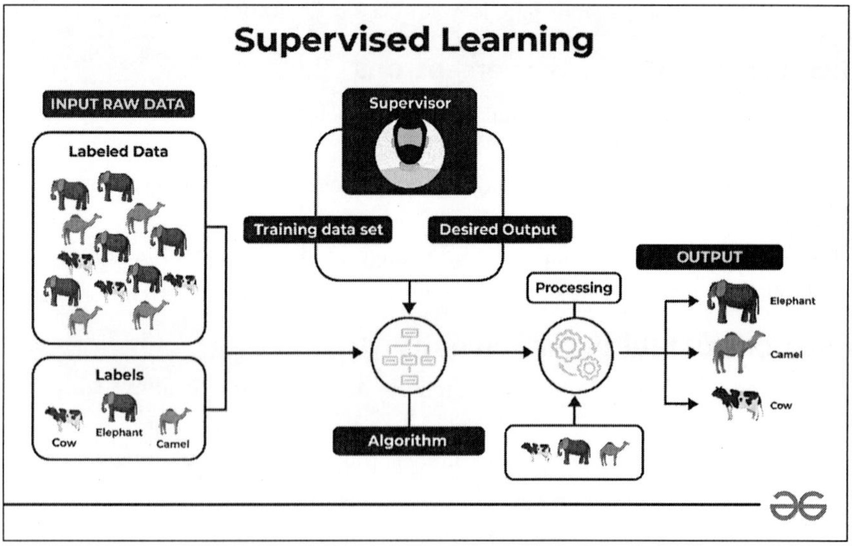


*Figure 2.12: Supervised Learning Model*

## Unsupervised Learning

Conversely, unsupervised learning operates on unlabeled data, indicating that the incoming data lacks predetermined classifications or anticipated outcomes.

Instead, the model identifies patterns, relationships, and structures within the dataset on its own.

Since there is no direct supervision, the algorithm explores the data, finding hidden structures and grouping similar data points together. For example, in customer segmentation, an unsupervised learning algorithm can analyze purchasing behaviors and group customers with similar interests, even without prior labels.

Both supervised and unsupervised learning play a crucial role in artificial intelligence, with supervised learning excelling in predictive tasks and unsupervised learning being valuable for discovering hidden insights in data.

## Types of Learning Under Supervision

Supervised learning algorithms can be categorized into two primary types: regression and classification. These approaches differ based on whether the output variable is continuous or categorical.

## What is Unsupervised Learning?

Unsupervised learning is a machine learning approach where the model learns without labeled data. Unlike supervised learning, there are no predefined categories or expected outputs. Instead, the algorithm identifies patterns, structures, and relationships within the dataset on its own.

In unsupervised learning, the model analyzes unclassified or unlabeled data and groups similar data points based on their characteristics. Since there is no direct supervision, the machine explores the dataset independently to find hidden structures and meaningful connections. For example, in customer segmentation, an unsupervised learning algorithm can group customers based on purchasing behavior without prior knowledge of predefined categories. Similarly, in anomaly detection, it can identify fraudulent transactions by recognizing unusual patterns.

Key unsupervised learning techniques include clustering.These methods help uncover insights from raw data without requiring labeled examples.

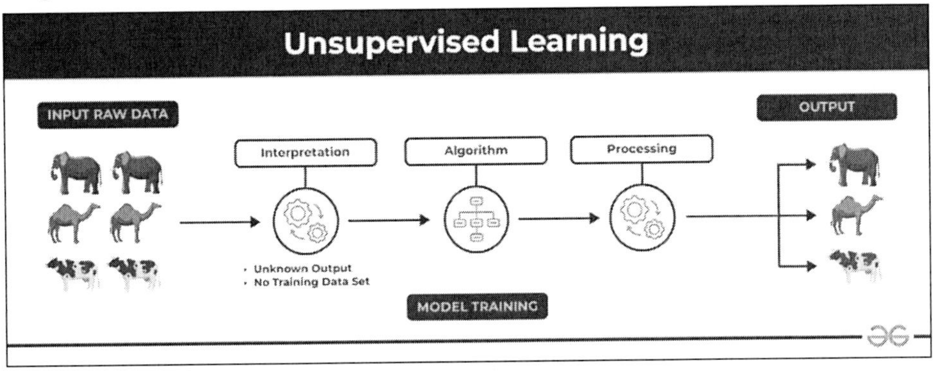


*Figure 2.13: Unsupervised Learning Model*

## 2.6 DEEP LEARNING ALGORITHMS

Deep learning is an advanced branch of artificial intelligence and machine learning that mimics human cognitive functions to analyze data and make intelligent decisions. It is particularly effective in handling complex and large-scale datasets by leveraging artificial neural networks.

Deep learning plays a vital role in predictive modeling, image recognition, speech processing, and natural language understanding. It relies on deep neural networks to process raw data and extract meaningful patterns. Unlike traditional machine learning, which struggles with high-dimensional data like images or videos, deep learning excels in such tasks.

### Why is Deep Learning Important?

Deep learning algorithms are essential for identifying intricate patterns and handling structured and unstructured data. Since they require vast amounts of data, deep learning models often outperform traditional machine learning in complex problem-solving.

For instance, ImageNet, a well-known deep learning tool, uses a dataset of over 14 million images to train models for image recognition. By analyzing thousands of labeled images, deep learning algorithms can detect objects, classify images, and even generate new visual content.

Deep learning networks process data through multiple layers. Each layer specializes in learning different features—from basic shapes and edges to complex objects like faces or animals. For example:

- Lower layers identify edges and textures in images.
- Middle layers recognize objects or patterns, like a dog's face.
- Higher layers understand broader categories, such as distinguishing between animals and humans.

### Deep Learning Algorithms

Several types of deep learning models are used across different applications.

#### Convolutional Neural Networks (CNNs)

CNNs, also known as ConvNets, are designed for image processing, pattern recognition, and object detection. Originally developed by Yann LeCun in 1998 under the name LeNet, CNNs were first used for digit recognition on postal codes.

CNNs are now widely used in:

- Anomaly detection (fraud detection in banking and cybersecurity)
- Satellite imagery analysis (classifying land use, tracking climate changes)
- Self-driving cars (object recognition and navigation)
- CNNs process images using multiple layers that extract features progressively. The convolutional layers detect edges and patterns, while the fully connected layers classify the final output. Their ability to learn hierarchical representations makes them highly effective for computer vision tasks.

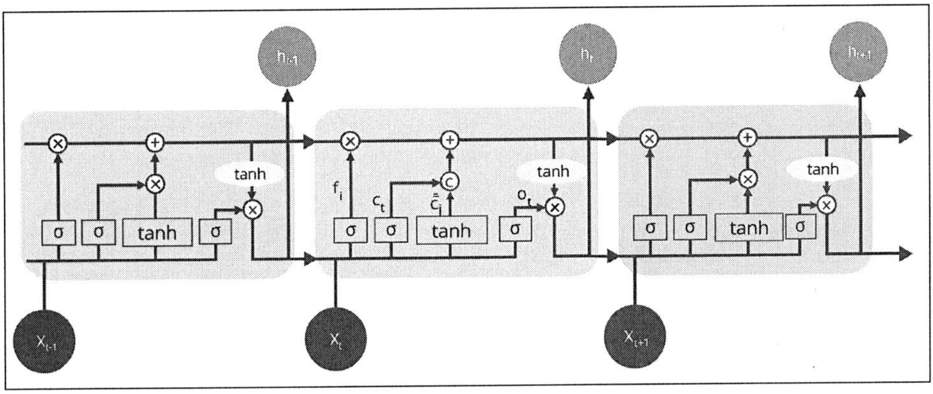


*Figure 2.14: Convolutional Neural Networks (CNNs)*

CNNs is responsible for applying convolutional operations to detect patterns such as edges, textures, and shapes. This layer also utilizes an activation function called the Rectified Linear Unit (ReLU), which enhances the feature map by eliminating negative values, ensuring only essential features are passed forward.

The Next Pooling Layer will lessen the spatial size of the retrieved feature maps in an attempt to fine-tune the features. Information is retained while computational power is reduced through a process known as pooling. Many pooling methods such as average pooling and max pooling, choose important elements from each region of the feature map to obtain.

Upon completing the steps of feature extraction, the information is put into a flat matrix of size m × 1. This data is now in a form ready to pass into a Fully Connected Layer, where an image is classified using learned features. In the end, a set of probability values indicating the chances of an image belonging to a specific class is generated.

## Long Short-Term Memory Networks (LSTMs)

LSTM networks are a distinct variant of Recurrent Neural Networks (RNNs) specifically engineered to analyze and learn from sequential input over prolonged durations. In contrast to conventional RNNs, which have difficulties with long-term dependencies because of the vanishing gradient issue, LSTMs incorporate a memory cell architecture that selectively maintains, modifies, or eliminates information via a gating mechanism. These networks have three essential gates: the forget gate, which ascertains which old knowledge to delete; the input gate, which determines what fresh information to retain; and the output gate, which governs the information transmitted as the final output. At each time step, the LSTM cell processes the input while preserving an internal cell state that transmits critical information ahead. The integration of sigmoid and tanh activation functions guarantees that the network proficiently acquires patterns from extended sequences. This architecture allows LSTMs to excel in applications related to sequential data, including voice recognition, time-series forecasting, language translation, and anomaly detection. LSTMs have transcended the constraints of conventional RNNs, establishing themselves as a crucial element in deep learning applications, enabling machines to comprehend and forecast intricate patterns in real-world data with greater precision.

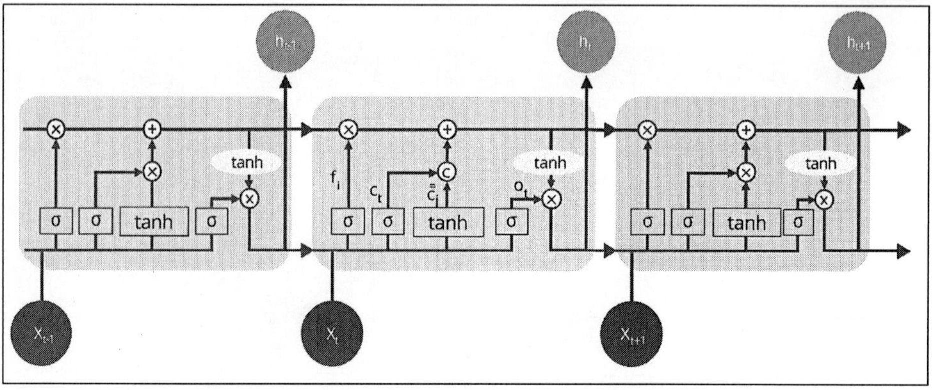


***Figure 2.15:*** *Long Short-Term Memory Networks (LSTMs)*

In RNNs, if time is represented as t, the output from time step t-1 is used as input for time step t. Similarly, the output at t serves as input for t+1, creating a sequence where each step influences the next. This cycle continues regardless of the input sequence length. Another advantage of RNNs is that they store past information efficiently, ensuring that the model size does not increase even as the data sequence grows. However, standard RNNs face challenges with long-term dependencies due to issues like the vanishing gradient problem, which LSTMs help mitigate.

## Generative Adversarial Networks (GANs)

GANs are a type of deep learning model used to generate new data that closely resembles a given dataset. They consist of two main components: a generator, which creates synthetic data, and a discriminator, which evaluates whether the generated data is real or fake. These two networks compete with each other, improving over time until the generator produces highly realistic outputs.

GANs have gained popularity in various applications, including enhancing astronomical images, simulating gravitational lensing effects, and improving video game graphics by upscaling textures to higher resolutions like 4K. They are also used to create realistic human faces, 3D objects, and animated characters. During training, the generator produces fake data, which the discriminator attempts to distinguish from real data. The process continues iteratively, refining both components until the generator can create convincing outputs that are difficult to differentiate from real data.

## Multilayer Perceptrons (MLPs)

MLPs are a fundamental component of deep learning and belong to the category of feedforward neural networks. They consist of multiple layers of perceptrons, each equipped with activation functions to process data. MLPs have a well-defined structure, including an input layer that receives raw data, one or more hidden layers that extract features and perform computations, and an output layer that generates predictions.

These networks are widely used in speech and image recognition, as well as language translation applications. The hidden layers enable MLPs to capture complex patterns in data, making them effective for a range of machine learning tasks. By leveraging multiple layers and activation functions, MLPs can model intricate relationships between inputs and outputs, playing a crucial role in modern artificial intelligence systems.

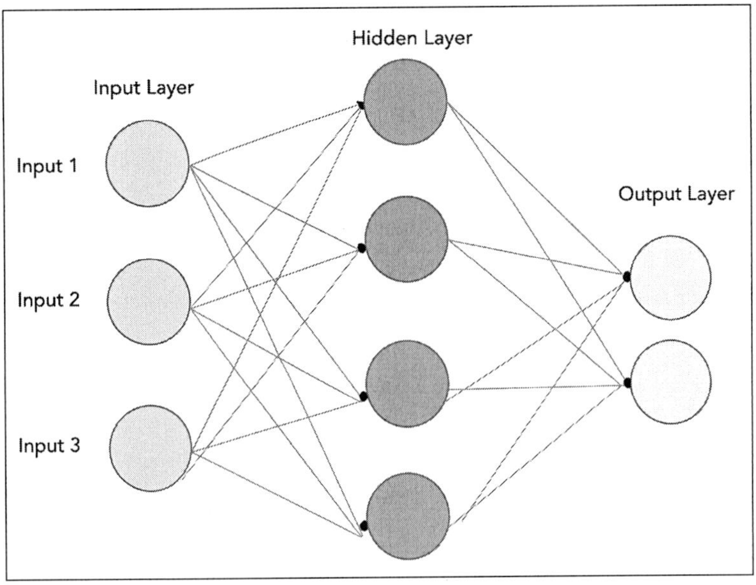


*Figure 2.16: Multilayer Perceptrons (MLPs)*

The operation of a Multilayer Perceptron (MLP) begins when data is introduced into the input layer. The neurons in this layer establish connections that flow in a single direction, forming a structured network. A weight difference exists between the input layer and the hidden layer, which influences how information is processed. MLPs utilize activation functions such as the sigmoid function, tanh function, and Rectified Linear Unit (ReLU) to determine which neurons should be activated during computation. These activation functions help the network identify relevant patterns and contribute to producing the desired output. MLPs are primarily used to train models by analyzing the relationships between different layers and how they interact with the given dataset.

## CASE STUDY

### *Artificial Neural Networks in Medical Diagnosis*

A hospital is implementing an Artificial Neural Network (ANN) to assist doctors in diagnosing diseases based on patient symptoms and medical history. The ANN is trained using a dataset containing past patient records, including test results and diagnoses.

## Discussion Questions

1. How can ANNs improve diagnostic accuracy in healthcare?
2. What challenges might arise when training the model with medical data?
3. How can the hospital ensure the ANN model remains reliable over time?

# Fuzzy Systems

UNIT 3

## 3.1 FUZZY LOGIC: CONCEPT, CHARACTERISTICS, AND ARCHITECTURE

Fuzzy logic deals with situations that are uncertain or ambiguous, where a statement may not be strictly true or false. In reality, many problems fall into a gray area, requiring more flexible solutions. Unlike traditional Boolean logic, which categorizes outcomes as either 0 (false) or 1 (true), fuzzy logic allows for a spectrum of truth values between 0 and 1. This approach enables more human-like decision-making by considering degrees of truth.

The concept of fuzzy logic was introduced by Lofti Zadeh in 1965 through the fuzzy set theory. Unlike computers, which operate in binary terms, humans tend to reason in shades of uncertainty. Fuzzy logic mimics this reasoning process, making it particularly useful in systems where precise inputs are not always available. It is commonly applied in microcontrollers, large network systems, and both hardware and software applications.

### Key Characteristics of Fuzzy Logic

A computational method called fuzzy logic handles ambiguous, imprecise, or uncertain data in a way that resembles human reasoning. Fuzzy logic uses degrees of truth instead of standard binary logic, which categorizes propositions as true or false (0 or 1), enabling a more adaptable and accurate depiction of real-world situations. Its foundation is fuzzy sets, where items may partially fall into several groups with membership values ranging from 0 to 1. Fuzzy logic is very helpful in decision-making systems because of this feature. It employs linguistic variables, enabling it to interpret qualitative data, such as "high temperature" or "moderate speed," instead of relying on rigid numerical thresholds. Additionally, fuzzy logic systems consist of rule-based structures that use "if-then" conditions to derive conclusions, making them adaptable and efficient in handling complex, uncertain environments. Due to its ability to approximate human decision-making, fuzzy logic is widely applied in fields such as automation, robotics, medical diagnosis, and consumer electronics, where precise mathematical models may not be feasible.

## 3.2 ARCHITECTURE OF A FUZZY LOGIC SYSTEM

A fuzzy logic system consists of four primary components, each playing a crucial role in decision-making:

- **Rule Base:** This component stores a set of If-Then conditions defined by experts to guide decision-making. Advancements in fuzzy logic have improved the accuracy and efficiency of rule-based systems, reducing ambiguity in the decision-making process.

- **Fuzzification:** This module converts crisp numerical inputs into fuzzy values. Sensors measure the input values, which are then transformed into fuzzy variables such as Small (S), Medium Positive (MP), Medium Negative (MN), Large Positive (LP), and Large Negative (LN) before further processing.
- **Inference Engine:** This component is the core of the fuzzy logic system, as it processes the input data and determines the relationship between rules and the current fuzzy inputs. It selects the most appropriate rule based on the input and applies it to generate control actions.
- **Defuzzification:** Once the inference engine processes the fuzzy values, the defuzzification module converts them back into crisp numerical outputs for final decision-making.

## 3.3 FUZZY SET THEORY

Fuzzy Set Theory framework model uncertainty, vagueness, and imprecision commonly found in real-world problems. It is particularly useful in fields such as artificial intelligence, control systems, and decision-making, where rigid boundaries are impractical. Fuzzy sets operate using membership functions, which define how each element's membership value is determined based on specific criteria. These functions allow for a smooth transition between categories rather than abrupt distinctions, making fuzzy set theory ideal for applications like medical diagnosis, image processing, and weather forecasting, where precise classifications are challenging. By providing a more human-like approach to handling uncertainty, fuzzy set theory has become an essential tool in various scientific and engineering disciplines.

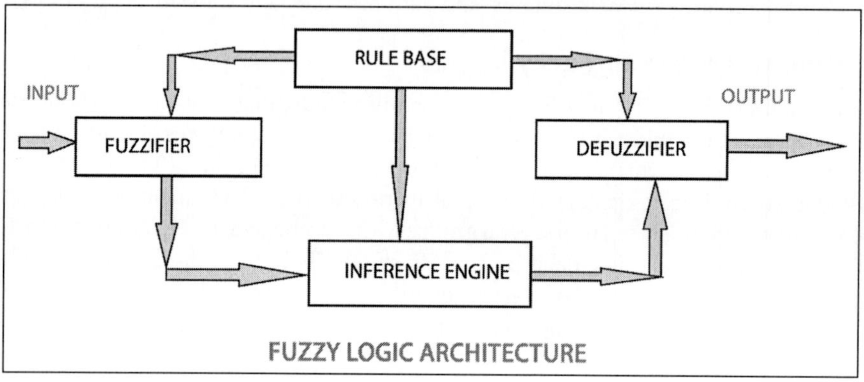


***Figure 3.1:*** *Fuzzy logic Architecture*

### Fuzzy Set Operations

This is the extend classical set theory by allowing partial membership of elements in a set. These operations include union, intersection, and complement, which are defined using membership functions that assign values between 0 and 1 to elements based on their degree of belonging. Below are the fundamental fuzzy set operations explained with an example:

#### 1. Union (Maximum Operation)

The union of two fuzzy sets A and B, denoted as $\mu_{A \cup B}(x)$, is determined by taking the maximum membership value of each element in both sets.

### *Formula*

$\mu_{AUB}(x) = \max(\mu_A(x), \mu_B(x))$

### *Example*

Let A and B be fuzzy sets with membership values:

- A = {(x1, 0.4), (x2, 0.7), (x3, 0.5)}
- B = {(x1, 0.6), (x2, 0.5), (x3, 0.8)}

The union is computed as:

- $\mu_{AUB}(x1) = \max(0.4, 0.6) = 0.6$
- $\mu_{AUB}(x2) = \max(0.7, 0.5) = 0.7$
- $\mu_{AUB}(x3) = \max(0.5, 0.8) = 0.8$

Thus, A ∪ B = {(x1, 0.6), (x2, 0.7), (x3, 0.8)}

## 2. Intersection (Minimum Operation)

The intersection of two fuzzy sets A and B, denoted as $\mu_{AUB}(x)$, is determined by taking the minimum membership value of each element in both sets.

### *Formula*

$\mu_{AUB}(x) = \min(\mu_A(x), \mu_B(x))$

### *Example*

Using the same sets A and B:

- $\mu_{AUB}(x1) = \min(0.4, 0.6) = 0.4$
- $\mu_{AUB}(x2) = \min(0.7, 0.5) = 0.5$
- $\mu_{AUB}(x3) = \min(0.5, 0.8) = 0.5$

Thus, A∪B = {(x1, 0.4), (x2, 0.5), (x3, 0.5)}

## 3. Complement

The complement of a fuzzy set A, denoted as $\mu_{A^c}(x)$, is calculated by subtracting each membership value from 1.

### *Formula*

$\mu_{A^c}(x) = 1 - \mu_A(x)$

### *Example*

For fuzzy set A:

- $\mu_{A^c}(x1) = 1 - 0.4 = 0.6$
- $\mu_{A^c}(x2) = 1 - 0.7 = 0.3$
- $\mu_{A^c}(x3) = 1 - 0.5 = 0.5$

Thus, $A^c$ = {(x1, 0.6), (x2, 0.3), (x3, 0.5)}

These fundamental fuzzy set operations are widely used in various applications, including decision-making systems, control engineering, and artificial intelligence, where uncertainty and imprecision must be accounted for.

## 3.4 FUZZY REASONING

Fuzzy reasoning is the process of making conclusions based on ambiguous and imprecise information by applying fuzzy logic. Fuzzy logic makes it possible to use fuzzy sets, which provide items varying degrees of membership, to describe ambiguous concepts. This is a thorough description of fuzzy reasoning complete with mathematical problems and solutions:

### Temperature Control System for a Greenhouse

#### Problem Statement

A greenhouse requires a temperature control system that decides when to activate the cooling mechanism. This decision depends on the current temperature and the preferred temperature range.

#### Solution Approach

##### *Defining Fuzzy Sets*

Let TT represent the current temperature and DD represent the desired temperature range.

Establish fuzzy sets for each:

TT can be classified as "cold," "cool," "warm," "hot," and "very hot," each with associated membership functions.

DD can be categorized as "low," "medium," and "high," also with membership functions.

#### Fuzzy Rule Formation

Develop fuzzy rules that connect TT and DD to the decision of activating the cooling system.

Example rules include:

- If TT is "hot" and DD is "low," activate the cooling system.
- If TT is "very hot" and DD is "medium," activate the cooling system.

#### Fuzzy Inference Process

Evaluate the given fuzzy rules based on the present values of TT and DD.

Combine the resulting outputs to determine the overall decision.

#### Defuzzification

Convert the fuzzy results into a precise decision using methods such as the centroid method or the maximum membership method.

##### *Example Scenario*

Suppose the current temperature is 30°C, and the desired range is 25-28°C. Given predefined membership functions, the fuzzy values can be determined as follows:

Membership values for TT:

"Cool" → 0.2

"Warm" → 0.8

"Hot" → 0.5

"Very Hot" → 0.1

Membership values for DD:

"Low" → 0.6

"Medium" → 0.4

"High" → 0.1

### Applying Fuzzy Rules

- **Rule 1:** Since TT = "hot" (0.5) and DD = "low" (0.6), the cooling system is triggered.
- **Rule 2:** Since TT = "very hot" (0.1) and DD = "medium" (0.4), the cooling system is also activated.

### Combining Rule Outputs

Since both rules support activating the cooling system, it increases the likelihood of switching it on.

### Defuzzification

Applying the centroid method results in a crisp decision, determining the precise cooling level required to maintain the preferred temperature range.

## 3.5 FUZZY INFERENCE SYSTEM

A Fuzzy Inference System (FIS) is a computational framework based on fuzzy logic principles that facilitate reasoning in environments characterized by uncertainty and imprecision. Unlike traditional binary logic systems that categorize inputs as either true or false, fuzzy logic operates with degrees of truth, enabling a more nuanced and flexible approach to decision-making. This adaptability makes FIS particularly useful in fields such as artificial intelligence, control systems, expert systems, and pattern recognition, where conventional mathematical models struggle to capture the complexity of real-world scenarios.

At its core, an FIS consists of four main components: fuzzification, a rule base, an inference engine, and defuzzification. The process begins with fuzzification, where crisp input values are transformed into fuzzy sets using membership functions. This step allows the system to handle imprecise data by representing variables in linguistic terms such as "low," "medium," and "high" rather than exact numerical values. Membership functions, which define the degree to which an input belongs to a fuzzy set, can take various shapes such as triangular, trapezoidal, Gaussian, or bell-shaped functions, depending on the desired level of precision and smoothness in transitions between states.

The second component, the rule base, consists of a collection of "if-then" rules that define how input variables relate to output variables. These rules, typically formulated by experts or derived from data, serve as the backbone of the decision-making process in an FIS. For example, in a temperature control system, a rule might state: "If the temperature is high, then the fan speed should be increased." The rule base captures human-like reasoning by translating vague concepts into structured logical statements that the system can process.

The inference engine is responsible for applying the rules from the rule base to the fuzzified inputs to generate fuzzy outputs. It evaluates the degree to which each rule is applicable based on the given input values and combines the results using fuzzy set operations such as min-max composition or product-sum composition. Two common inference methods used in FIS are the Mamdani and Sugeno methods. The Mamdani approach, named after Ebrahim Mamdani, uses fuzzy sets for both inputs and outputs, making it intuitive and widely used in control applications. The Sugeno method, on the other hand, represents outputs as linear functions of input variables, making it computationally efficient and suitable for optimization problems.

Once the inference engine has processed the rules and derived a fuzzy output, the final step is defuzzification. This process converts the fuzzy output back into a crisp numerical value to facilitate decision-making in real-world applications. Several defuzzification techniques exist, including the centroid method (which finds the center of mass of the fuzzy set), the maximum membership principle (which selects the output with the highest membership value), and the weighted average method. The choice of defuzzification method depends on the specific application and the desired level of precision.

FIS is widely applied in various domains due to its ability to handle imprecise data and make decisions in uncertain environments. One notable application is in control systems, where fuzzy logic controllers (FLCs) are used to regulate processes such as temperature, speed, and pressure. Unlike traditional proportional-integral-derivative (PID) controllers that rely on precise mathematical models, FLCs use linguistic rules to adjust system behavior dynamically, resulting in smoother and more adaptive control. For instance, in an air conditioning system, an FLC can adjust cooling levels based on factors such as room temperature, humidity, and user preferences, leading to improved comfort and energy efficiency.

Another prominent application of FIS is in medical diagnosis and decision support systems. Medical data often involve uncertainties due to variations in patient conditions, measurement errors, and subjective interpretations by healthcare professionals. FIS helps in modeling such uncertainties by incorporating expert knowledge into fuzzy rule-based systems. For example, a fuzzy-based diagnostic system can evaluate symptoms such as fever, cough, and fatigue to determine the likelihood of a disease, providing doctors with valuable insights for diagnosis and treatment planning.

In artificial intelligence and machine learning, FIS plays a crucial role in pattern recognition and classification tasks. By leveraging fuzzy rules and membership functions, FIS can classify objects, recognize speech patterns, and analyze images even when input data is noisy or incomplete. A common example is handwriting recognition, where fuzzy logic enables systems to interpret handwritten characters despite variations in writing styles and distortions. Similarly, in speech recognition applications, FIS helps process ambiguous audio signals to improve accuracy in understanding spoken commands.

The financial sector also benefits from FIS in areas such as stock market analysis, risk assessment, and credit scoring. Traditional financial models often struggle with market volatility and unpredictable economic trends, but FIS provides a flexible approach by incorporating expert opinions and historical data into decision-making processes. For instance, a fuzzy-based trading system can assess factors such as market sentiment, historical price trends, and economic indicators to generate investment recommendations with greater adaptability to changing market conditions.

Automotive applications have also embraced FIS, particularly in areas such as driver assistance systems and autonomous vehicles. Modern cars use fuzzy logic for functions such as adaptive cruise control, braking assistance, and lane-keeping systems. These systems rely on fuzzy rules to make real-time decisions based on sensor data, ensuring smoother and safer driving experiences. For example, an adaptive cruise control system can adjust vehicle speed based on factors such as traffic flow and road conditions, enhancing both safety and fuel efficiency.

Despite its numerous advantages, FIS also has some limitations. One major challenge is the design of an appropriate rule base, which requires expert knowledge and careful tuning of membership functions. Additionally, FIS can become computationally complex when dealing with a large number of input variables and rules. These hybrid systems leverage the learning capabilities of machine learning models while retaining the interpretability of fuzzy logic, leading to more robust and efficient decision-making systems.

In conclusion, a Fuzzy Inference System is a powerful tool for modeling and decision-making in uncertain environments. By incorporating human-like reasoning through fuzzy logic, FIS enables applications in diverse fields such as control systems, medical diagnostics, artificial intelligence, finance, and automotive systems. Its ability to handle imprecise data, adapt to changing conditions, and integrate expert knowledge makes it a valuable approach for solving complex real-world problems. However, designing effective FIS requires careful consideration of rule selection, membership function tuning, and computational efficiency. With ongoing advancements in artificial intelligence and data science, FIS continues to evolve, contributing to smarter and more adaptive technologies in various domains.

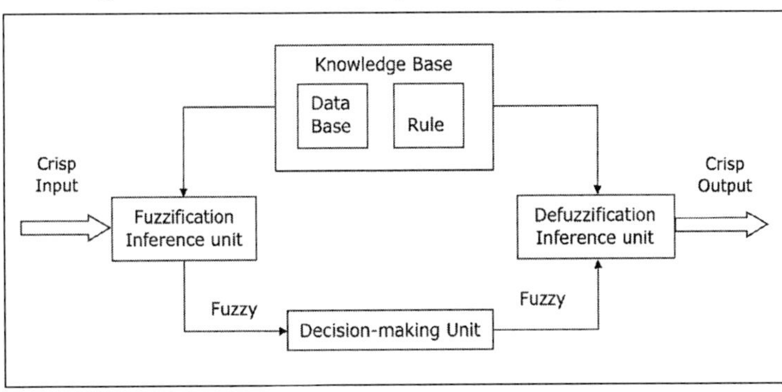


***Figure 3.2:** Fuzzy Inference System Architecture*

## Mamdani Fuzzy Inference System

The Mamdani Fuzzy Inference System was introduced in 1975 by Ebrahim Mamdani. It was initially developed to regulate a steam engine and boiler system by formulating fuzzy rules based on expert knowledge from individuals working with the system.

### Steps to Compute the Output

To determine the output of this FIS, the following steps are followed:

- **Define Fuzzy Rules:** Identify a set of fuzzy rules that will guide the inference process.
- **Fuzzification of Inputs:** Convert crisp input values into fuzzy values using the input membership functions.
- **Compute Rule Strength:** Combine the fuzzified inputs based on the fuzzy rules to determine rule strength.

- **Determine Consequent Output:** Apply the rule strength to the output membership functions to generate rule consequents.
- **Aggregate Outputs:** Combine all rule consequents to form the overall output distribution.
- **Defuzzification:** Convert the fuzzy output distribution into a crisp value to obtain the final result.

This structured approach enables the Mamdani FIS to handle complex decision-making processes effectively.

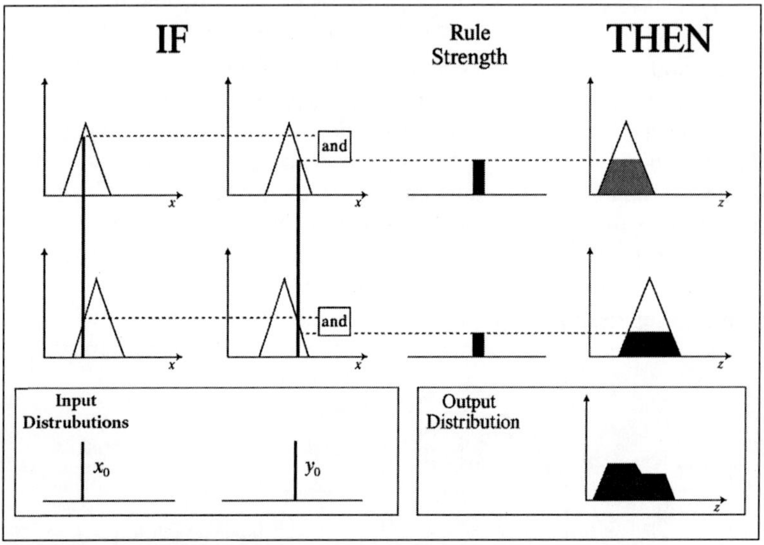


***Figure 3.3:*** *Mamdani Fuzzy Inference System*

## Takagi-Sugeno Fuzzy Model (TS Method)

The Takagi-Sugeno Fuzzy Model was introduced in 1985 by Takagi, Sugeno, and Kang. The rule structure follows the format:

IF $x$ is $A$ AND $y$ is $B$, THEN $Z = f(x, y)$

Here, A and B represent fuzzy sets in the antecedent, while Z is a crisp function in the consequent, typically expressed as a linear function of the inputs.

## Fuzzy Inference Process in the TS Method

The Takagi-Sugeno fuzzy inference process follows these steps:

- **Fuzzification of Inputs:** Convert the system's input values into fuzzy values.
- **Applying Fuzzy Operators:** Use fuzzy logic operations to determine the output.

## Sugeno Rule Format

The rule format in the Sugeno Model is given as:

IF $x = 7$ AND $y = 9$, THEN output is Z = ax + by + c

## Comparison: Mamdani vs. Sugeno Model

The Mamdani and Sugeno models differ in several ways:

- **Output Membership Function:** The Sugeno model uses either a linear or constant output function, unlike Mamdani's fuzzy output membership function.
- **Aggregation & Defuzzification:** The Sugeno model has a different aggregation and defuzzification approach due to its distinct rule consequences.
- **Mathematical Formulation:** The Sugeno method involves more mathematical equations compared to the Mamdani model.
- **Adjustable Parameters:** The Sugeno controller has more tunable parameters, providing greater flexibility than the Mamdani controller.

This makes the Sugeno model particularly useful in control applications requiring precise and computationally efficient outputs.

## Deep Learning Architecture for Fuzzy Logic or Fuzzy Neural Network

### Neuro-Fuzzy Systems: A Hybrid Approach

Neuro-fuzzy systems represent a hybrid approach that combines the strengths of fuzzy logic and artificial neural networks (ANNs) to create more efficient and adaptive decision-making models. This integration leverages the interpretability of fuzzy logic with the learning capability of neural networks, making neuro-fuzzy systems highly effective in handling complex problems that involve uncertainty, imprecision, and non-linearity. The primary motivation behind this hybrid approach is to overcome the limitations of each individual technique: while fuzzy logic excels in dealing with human-like reasoning and linguistic rules, it lacks self-learning capabilities; conversely, neural networks are excellent at learning from data but function as black-box models that are difficult to interpret. By fusing these two paradigms, neuro-fuzzy systems can learn from data while maintaining an interpretable structure, making them suitable for a wide range of applications, including control systems, pattern recognition, medical diagnostics, financial forecasting, and robotics.

A neuro-fuzzy system primarily consists of a fuzzy inference system (FIS) that is enhanced with learning mechanisms borrowed from artificial neural networks. The structure of a neuro-fuzzy system typically includes input and output layers, membership function layers, rule base layers, and a learning algorithm that adjusts parameters to optimize performance. The learning process in neuro-fuzzy systems is generally accomplished using supervised or unsupervised learning techniques, often inspired by backpropagation, gradient descent, or evolutionary algorithms. The most commonly used neuro-fuzzy model is the Adaptive Neuro-Fuzzy Inference System (ANFIS), which was introduced to enhance the adaptability of fuzzy systems by employing neural network-based training methods.

In traditional fuzzy systems, designing an appropriate rule base requires expert knowledge, which can be time-consuming and subjective. Neuro-fuzzy models eliminate this dependence on domain expertise by learning from empirical data, making them more robust and scalable for real-world applications. Furthermore, these systems can adapt to changing environments by continuously updating their parameters, allowing them to improve performance over time without requiring manual intervention.

In control systems, neuro-fuzzy techniques have been widely used to enhance process automation and intelligent decision-making. For instance, in industrial automation, neuro-fuzzy controllers are employed to optimize complex processes such as temperature regulation, motor control, and chemical processing. Traditional control methods often struggle with uncertain and nonlinear systems, but neuro-fuzzy controllers adaptively learn system behaviors and adjust parameters accordingly, resulting in improved accuracy and efficiency. Similarly, in robotics, neuro-fuzzy algorithms enable autonomous systems to make real-time decisions based on sensor data, enhancing navigation, object recognition, and motion planning capabilities.

Medical diagnostics and healthcare applications have also benefited from neuro-fuzzy systems due to their ability to handle uncertain and imprecise medical data. In diagnostic decision support systems, neuro-fuzzy models assist healthcare professionals by analyzing patient symptoms, medical histories, and test results to generate accurate diagnoses. These systems can learn from historical patient data and improve over time, providing personalized recommendations and reducing diagnostic errors. For example, neuro-fuzzy algorithms have been used in cancer detection, cardiovascular disease prediction, and medical image analysis, demonstrating their effectiveness in handling complex medical scenarios.

Another significant application of neuro-fuzzy systems is in financial forecasting and risk assessment. The financial market is highly volatile, with numerous uncertain variables influencing stock prices, interest rates, and economic trends. Traditional mathematical models often fail to capture these uncertainties, but neuro-fuzzy approaches offer a more flexible and adaptive solution. By learning from historical financial data and integrating expert knowledge through fuzzy rules, neuro-fuzzy systems can predict stock market trends, optimize investment strategies, and assess credit risks with greater accuracy. Banks and financial institutions leverage these models to enhance fraud detection, loan approval processes, and algorithmic trading strategies.

In the field of pattern recognition and machine learning, neuro-fuzzy models have proven to be effective in tasks such as handwriting recognition, speech processing, and image classification. Unlike conventional machine learning models that rely solely on numerical data, neuro-fuzzy systems can interpret linguistic and ambiguous information, making them suitable for real-world recognition tasks. For instance, in speech recognition applications, neuro-fuzzy algorithms can process variations in pronunciation, accents, and background noise, improving the accuracy of voice-controlled systems. Similarly, in image processing, these models help in feature extraction, segmentation, and object recognition by leveraging both fuzzy rules and neural network learning capabilities.

The integration of neuro-fuzzy systems with deep learning and evolutionary computation has further expanded their potential in artificial intelligence applications. Hybrid models combining neuro-fuzzy techniques with deep neural networks (DNNs) have been explored to improve decision-making in autonomous systems, such as self-driving cars and smart grids. These advanced models use deep learning to extract complex patterns from large datasets while incorporating fuzzy logic for reasoning and interpretability. Additionally, evolutionary algorithms such as genetic algorithms and particle swarm optimization have been employed to optimize neuro-fuzzy system parameters, enhancing their adaptability and efficiency.

Despite their numerous advantages, neuro-fuzzy systems also present some challenges. Additionally, determining the optimal number of fuzzy rules and membership functions can be challenging, as an excessive number of rules may lead to overfitting, while too few rules may result in poor generalization. To address these challenges, researchers have developed various optimization techniques, including pruning redundant rules, feature selection methods, and hybrid learning approaches that combine different machine learning techniques.

Looking ahead, the future of neuro-fuzzy systems appears promising, with ongoing research focused on improving their scalability, interpretability, and real-time processing capabilities. The integration of neuro-fuzzy techniques with edge computing and Internet of Things (IoT) applications is expected to drive innovations in smart cities, healthcare monitoring, and industrial automation. Additionally, advances in neuromorphic computing and quantum computing may further enhance the efficiency of neuro-fuzzy models, opening new possibilities for intelligent decision-making systems in various domains.

In conclusion, neuro-fuzzy systems represent a powerful hybrid approach that combines the best aspects of fuzzy logic and neural networks to address complex, uncertain, and nonlinear problems. By integrating data-driven learning with human-like reasoning, these models offer a flexible and adaptive solution for a wide range of applications, including control systems, medical diagnostics, financial forecasting, pattern recognition, and artificial intelligence. While challenges such as computational complexity and rule optimization remain, ongoing advancements in machine learning and optimization techniques continue to enhance the performance and applicability of neuro-fuzzy systems. As technology evolves, neuro-fuzzy models will play an increasingly vital role in shaping intelligent and autonomous systems capable of making sophisticated decisions in dynamic environments.

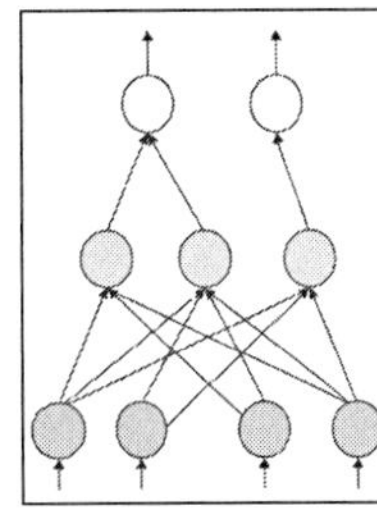

***Figure 3.4:*** *Structure of a Neuro-Fuzzy System*

The structure of a neuro-fuzzy system consists of five main layers that work together to process input data and generate accurate outputs. The first layer, known as the input layer, receives raw data and passes it to the next stage. The second layer consists of fuzzy membership functions that convert crisp inputs into fuzzy values by determining their degree of belonging to predefined categories. The third layer represents the fuzzy rule base, where predefined rules define how inputs should be processed. In the fourth layer, a neural network helps fine-tune these rules and adjust membership functions dynamically based on training data. Finally, the output layer defuzzifies the results, converting them back into meaningful numerical values for decision-making. This structured approach allows neuro-fuzzy systems to adapt and improve over time, making them highly effective in handling uncertainty and complex decision-making tasks across various fields.

## Cooperative Fuzzy Neural Network (CFNN)

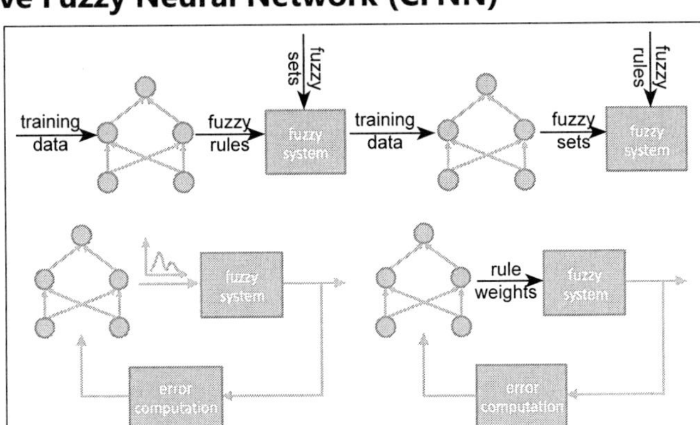


***Figure 3.5:*** *Architecture of CFNN*

A CFNN is a hybrid computational model that combines ANNs and fuzzy logic systems, where both components operate independently while complementing each other's strengths. In this approach, the neural network learns parameters from the fuzzy system, helping to refine fuzzy rules, membership functions, or decision-making processes. Unlike other hybrid models, such as concurrent or fully integrated fuzzy neural networks, CFNNs maintain a clear separation between the fuzzy and neural components, allowing for flexibility in learning and adaptation.

## Core Working Principle of CFNN

CFNNs operate based on a collaborative learning mechanism, where the neural network primarily acts as a learning mechanism for the fuzzy system. This cooperation can occur in two ways:

- **Offline Learning:** The ANN learns fuzzy rules and membership functions from training data before the fuzzy system is deployed. This process ensures that the fuzzy system starts with optimized parameters.
- **Online Learning:** The neural network continuously refines the fuzzy system's parameters during real-time operation, adapting to changing conditions.

In both cases, the ANN does not replace the fuzzy system but assists in parameter tuning, learning from data, and optimizing rule sets. The fuzzy system, in turn, provides a structured decision-making framework that enhances the interpretability of the neural network.

## Architectural Components of CFNN

A Cooperative Fuzzy Neural Network consists of several key components that work together to process input data and generate outputs efficiently:

- **Fuzzy System:** Defines linguistic variables and membership functions.
  - Uses if-then fuzzy rules for decision-making.
  - Provides a structured framework for handling imprecise or uncertain data.
- **Artificial Neural Network (ANN):** Learns from training data to optimize the fuzzy system.
  - Adjusts membership functions, rule weights, or even constructs fuzzy rules.
  - Enhances the adaptability of the system by allowing it to learn from real-world data.
- **Fuzzification Layer:** Converts crisp numerical inputs into fuzzy values using predefined membership functions.
- **Inference Engine:** Processes the fuzzy rules and applies inference mechanisms to derive results.
  - The ANN helps modify rule strengths dynamically.
- **Defuzzification Layer:** Converts the fuzzy output back into a crisp numerical value for decision-making.

## Types of Cooperative Fuzzy Neural Networks

Different variations of CFNNs exist, each designed to address specific challenges in fuzzy-neural integration:

- **Fuzzy Set Learning CFNN:** The neural network learns membership functions from training data.
  - Membership functions are adjusted offline, and fuzzy rules remain predefined.
- **Fuzzy Rule Learning CFNN:** The ANN derives fuzzy rules from training data using clustering techniques.
  - This method helps when expert-defined fuzzy rules are unavailable.
- **Online Membership Function Learning CFNN:** The ANN continuously refines membership function parameters during real-time operation.
  - This approach is useful in dynamic environments where data patterns change over time.
- **Rule Weight Learning CFNN:** The neural network assigns importance to fuzzy rules by adjusting rule weights.
  - This improves decision accuracy by prioritizing more relevant rules.

## Advantages of CFNN

CFNNs offer a range of benefits that make them suitable for complex, real-world applications:

- **Improved Adaptability:** The ANN enables real-time learning, allowing the system to adjust to new data patterns.
- **Enhanced Interpretability:** Unlike traditional neural networks, the fuzzy system maintains a structured, human-readable decision-making process.
- **Robustness to Uncertainty:** Fuzzy logic helps handle imprecise, noisy, or incomplete data effectively.
- **Efficient Parameter Optimization:** The ANN automates the tuning of fuzzy parameters, reducing reliance on manual adjustments.
- **Scalability:** CFNNs can be scaled to handle complex systems with numerous input variables.

## Applications of Cooperative Fuzzy Neural Networks

- **Industrial Process Control:** Used in automated manufacturing systems and robotics to fine-tune fuzzy control parameters.
- **Medical Diagnosis and Healthcare:** Applied in disease prediction models and patient monitoring systems to analyze medical data effectively.
- **Financial Forecasting:** Used for stock market prediction, risk analysis, and fraud detection by learning financial trends.
- **Cybersecurity and Anomaly Detection:** Helps detect network intrusions, malware, and fraudulent activities by recognizing unusual patterns in data.

## Challenges and Future Directions

While CFNNs offer several advantages, they also pose certain challenges:

- **Computational Complexity:** The integration of ANN and fuzzy systems increases processing time and resource requirements.
- **Parameter Tuning Issues:** Finding the right balance between fuzzy logic and ANN learning remains a complex task.

Future research in deep learning, reinforcement learning, and quantum computing may help improve CFNNs by making them more efficient, scalable, and capable of handling higher-dimensional data. The continued development of explainable AI (XAI) techniques may also enhance the transparency of CFNN-based decision systems, ensuring they remain interpretable and trustworthy.

## Hybrid Fuzzy Neural Network (HFNN)

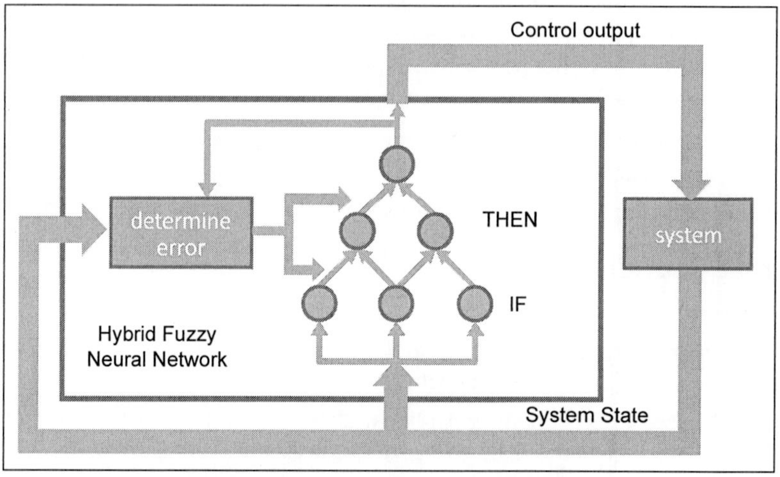


***Figure 3.6:*** *A hybrid fuzzy neural network*

A HFNN is an advanced computational model that integrates fuzzy logic systems with ANNs to enhance learning efficiency, adaptability, and interpretability. Unlike cooperative and concurrent models, which keep neural and fuzzy components separate or allow them to function in parallel, HFNNs fully integrate both frameworks into a unified system. By doing so, HFNNs address key challenges associated with each method when used individually, such as the black-box nature of ANNs and the heuristic tuning required for fuzzy systems.

## Fundamental Concepts and Structure of HFNN

The core idea behind HFNNs is to enable data-driven learning while preserving human-interpretable fuzzy rules. Traditional fuzzy systems require expert-defined rules, making them difficult to scale when dealing with large, complex datasets. HFNNs solve these issues by automatically generating or refining fuzzy rules based on learning patterns within data.

The structure of an HFNN typically consists of the following layers:

- **Input Layer:** This layer receives crisp numerical inputs from external sources, such as sensor data or user inputs. These values are then transformed into fuzzy variables using membership functions.
- **Fuzzification Layer:** This layer maps crisp inputs into fuzzy values by applying predefined membership functions (e.g., triangular, trapezoidal, or Gaussian).
- **Rule Layer:** This layer represents fuzzy rules, which define relationships between input and output variables. The ANN component helps adjust rule parameters dynamically.

- **Inference Layer:** This layer processes the fuzzy rules to determine the degree to which each rule applies to the current input values. The network assigns weights and adjusts parameters using training data.
- **Defuzzification Layer:** Once fuzzy inference is performed, this layer converts fuzzy outputs into crisp numerical values using techniques like the centroid method or max membership principle.
- **Output Layer:** The final layer produces the system's decision, prediction, or classification result based on the processed information.

## Learning Mechanism in HFNNs

HFNNs utilize neural learning algorithms to optimize fuzzy rule parameters, membership functions, and inference mechanisms. The learning process can be supervised, unsupervised, or reinforcement-based, depending on the application. Some common learning techniques include:

- **Gradient Descent:** Used to update parameters in backpropagation-based HFNN models.
- **Genetic Algorithms (GAs):** Applied to optimize fuzzy rule selection and structure evolution.
- **Hybrid Optimization:** Combining multiple learning techniques to balance accuracy, interpretability, and computational efficiency.

## Advantages of Hybrid Fuzzy Neural Networks

HFNNs offer several benefits over traditional fuzzy logic systems and neural networks:

- **Enhanced Interpretability:** The fuzzy component ensures that the system remains explainable, unlike standard neural networks, which act as black-box models.
- **Data-Driven Learning:** The neural component allows HFNNs to learn and adapt automatically, reducing reliance on manually crafted rules.
- **Robustness to Uncertainty:** Fuzzy logic helps handle imprecise or noisy data, making HFNNs well-suited for real-world applications.
- **Improved Generalization:** By incorporating both rule-based reasoning and pattern recognition, HFNNs achieve better generalization in complex problem domains.
- **Dynamic Adaptation:** HFNNs can update fuzzy rules and membership functions over time as new data becomes available.

## Applications of HFNNs

Due to their versatility, HFNNs have been successfully applied in various domains, including:

- **Industrial Control Systems:** Used for intelligent automation, adaptive control of manufacturing processes, and robotic systems.
- **Medical Diagnosis:** Applied in disease prediction, patient monitoring, and medical image processing.
- **Financial Forecasting:** Helps in stock market prediction, risk analysis, and credit scoring.

- **Natural Language Processing (NLP):** Improves sentiment analysis, text classification, and speech recognition.
- **Autonomous Vehicles:** Enhances decision-making in self-driving cars through real-time sensor fusion.
- **Cybersecurity:** Detects anomalies in network traffic, preventing fraud and cyber threats.

## Challenges and Future Directions

Despite their advantages, HFNNs face some challenges:

- **Computational Complexity:** The integration of fuzzy logic and neural learning increases computational requirements.
- **Rule Explosion:** As input dimensions increase, the number of fuzzy rules can grow exponentially, requiring efficient rule pruning techniques.
- **Parameter Tuning:** Balancing accuracy and interpretability remains an open research problem.
- **Scalability:** Extending HFNNs to large-scale datasets requires optimization strategies like deep learning hybridization.

Future advancements in deep learning, quantum computing, and bio-inspired algorithms may further enhance the capabilities of HFNNs, making them more efficient, scalable, and interpretable for next-generation intelligent systems.

## CASE STUDY

A company wants to develop a smart washing machine that can automatically adjust the wash cycle based on the level of dirt in clothes, water temperature, and fabric type. Instead of using fixed rules, the company decides to implement a fuzzy logic system to determine the optimal washing time.

## Discussion Question

How can a fuzzy inference system be designed to optimize the washing time based on the following input parameters?

- **Dirt Level:** (Low, Medium, High)
- **Water Temperature:** (Cold, Warm, Hot)
- **Fabric Type:** (Delicate, Normal, Heavy)

What would be the necessary fuzzy sets, rule base, and defuzzification method to determine the appropriate washing time? Provide a step-by-step explanation of how the fuzzy system would process these inputs to generate an efficient wash cycle.

4

# Genetic Algorithms

UNIT

## 4.1 INTRODUCTION TO GENETIC ALGORITHMS

Genetic Algorithms (GAs) are a type of optimization technique inspired by the principles of natural selection and genetics. First introduced by John Holland in the 1970s, GAs mimic the process of evolution to solve complex optimization and search problems. They are widely used in artificial intelligence, engineering, bioinformatics, finance, and other domains requiring efficient problem-solving methods.

### What are Genetic Algorithms?

Genetic Algorithms are a class of evolutionary algorithms that work by evolving a population of potential solutions over multiple generations. They apply the concepts of selection, crossover, and mutation to improve solutions iteratively. The main objective is to find the best or near-optimal solution for a given problem.

### Key Components of Genetic Algorithms

Genetic Algorithms operate using several key components:

- **Population:** A set of potential solutions to the problem. Each individual in the population is called a chromosome and represents a candidate solution.
- **Chromosomes:** Encoded representations of possible solutions, often represented as binary strings, real numbers, or permutations.
- **Fitness Function:** A mathematical function used to evaluate how well a given chromosome solves the problem. Higher fitness values indicate better solutions.
- **Selection:** A process that chooses the best individuals for reproduction based on their fitness scores. Common selection methods include:
  - Roulette Wheel Selection
  - Tournament Selection

### Rank-Based Selection

- **Crossover (Recombination):** A genetic operation where two parent solutions exchange genetic material to create offspring. This helps in exploring new solutions.
- **Mutation:** A random change introduced in offspring to maintain genetic diversity and prevent premature convergence to suboptimal solutions.
- **Termination Condition:** The algorithm stops when a predefined criterion is met, such as reaching a maximum number of generations or finding an optimal solution.

### How Genetic Algorithms Work

The working of Genetic Algorithms follows these steps:

- **Initialization:** Generate an initial population of possible solutions randomly.
- **Evaluation:** Compute the fitness of each individual in the population using the fitness function.
- **Selection:** Choose the best individuals to be parents based on their fitness values.
- **Crossover:** Combine selected parents to create new offspring.
- **Mutation:** Apply small random changes to offspring to maintain diversity.
- **Replacement:** Form a new population by replacing old individuals with new offspring.
- **Repeat:** The process continues until the termination condition is met.

### Applications of Genetic Algorithms

Genetic Algorithms have been successfully applied in various domains, including:

- **Optimization Problems:** Used in scheduling, route planning, and logistics.
- **Machine Learning:** Feature selection and hyperparameter tuning.
- **Bioinformatics:** DNA sequence alignment and protein structure prediction.
- **Finance:** Portfolio optimization and stock market predictions.
- **Robotics:** Motion planning and control system design.

## 4.2 GENETIC ALGORITHM SEARCH SPACE AND REPRESENTATION

### Search Space in Genetic Algorithms

The search space in Genetic Algorithms (GAs) refers to the entire set of possible solutions that the algorithm explores to find the optimal solution to a given problem. Each point in this space represents a candidate solution, and the goal of the GA is to navigate this space efficiently using selection, crossover, and mutation.

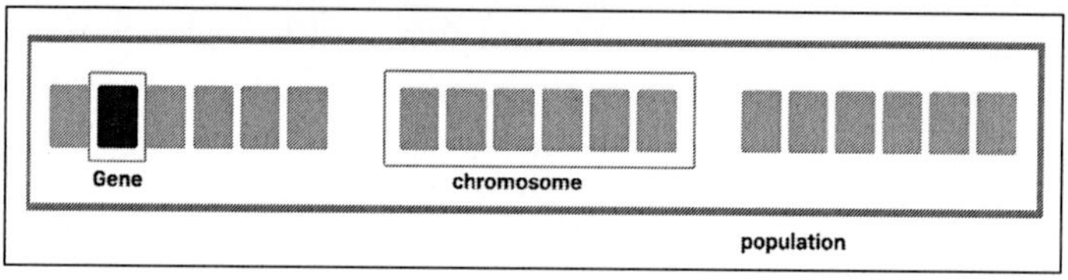


*Fig. 4.1*

### Characteristics of Search Space

1. **Dimensionality:** The number of variables influencing the solution.
2. **Feasibility:** Some regions of the search space contain feasible solutions, while others do not.
3. **Fitness Landscape:** Represents how fitness values change across different points in the search space.
4. **Exploration vs. Exploitation:** The algorithm balances searching new areas (exploration) and refining existing solutions (exploitation).

## Example: Search Space Representation

*Table 4.1: Representation in Genetic Algorithms*

| Solution Representation | Binary String | Real-Value Encoding | Permutation |
|---|---|---|---|
| Solution 1 | 11001011 | [1.2, 2.3, 3.5] | (A, B, C, D) |
| Solution 2 | 10110110 | [4.1, 5.6, 1.9] | (B, A, D, C) |
| Solution 3 | 11100011 | [2.8, 3.7, 4.2] | (C, D, A, B) |

Representation in Genetic Algorithms refers to how solutions (chromosomes) are encoded. The effectiveness of a GA depends on selecting an appropriate representation method for the problem being solved.

## Types of Representation

### *1. Binary Representation*

In this method, solutions are encoded as binary strings (0s and 1s). This representation is widely used due to its simplicity.

#### *Example*

**Chromosome:** 11001011 (represents a specific solution).

### *2. Real-Valued Representation*

Instead of binary encoding, solutions are represented as real-valued vectors. This is useful for optimization problems involving continuous variables.

#### *Example*

**Chromosome:** [3.14, 2.71, 1.62]

### *3. Permutation Representation*

This method is used in problems where the order of elements matters, such as the Traveling Salesman Problem (TSP).

#### *Example*

**Chromosome:** (A, B, C, D)

*Table 4.2: Comparison of Representation Methods*

| Representation Type | Used For | Advantages | Disadvantages |
|---|---|---|---|
| Binary | Combinatorial Optimization | Simple, easy crossover | Not suitable for continuous values |
| Real-Valued | Continuous Optimization | Efficient for real-world problems | Requires specialized operators |
| Permutation | Order-Based Problems | Ensures valid permutations | Complex crossover and mutation |

## Survival of the Fittest in Genetic Algorithms

The concept of Survival of the Fittest originates from Charles Darwin's theory of evolution, which suggests that individuals best adapted to their environment have a higher chance of survival and reproduction. In Genetic Algorithms (GAs), this concept is fundamental to the optimization process, ensuring that stronger solutions are more likely to pass their genetic material to subsequent generations.

### Understanding Survival of the Fittest

In the context of Genetic Algorithms, Survival of the Fittest refers to the principle that solutions with higher fitness scores are more likely to be selected for reproduction, thereby improving the overall quality of solutions over successive generations. The fitness of an individual is determined by a predefined fitness function, which evaluates how well a candidate solution meets the optimization criteria.

### Role of Fitness Function in Survival

The fitness function plays a crucial role in implementing the concept of Survival of the Fittest. It quantifies how well each solution solves the problem at hand. Individuals with higher fitness values are given a greater chance of selection for reproduction, while weaker individuals are either eliminated or have a reduced probability of passing their traits to the next generation.

For example, in a traveling salesman problem, a fitness function might be designed to minimize the total distance traveled. Solutions with shorter routes will have higher fitness and a better chance of being selected for reproduction.

### Selection Methods Promoting Survival of the Fittest

Several selection strategies ensure that the fittest individuals are more likely to survive and propagate their genes. Some of the most common selection methods include:

- **Roulette Wheel Selection:** Assigns a probability of selection based on fitness values.
  - Higher fitness solutions have a greater chance of being chosen.
- **Tournament Selection:** Randomly selects a subset of individuals from the population.
  - The fittest individual from the subset is chosen for reproduction.
- **Rank-Based Selection:** Instead of selecting based on absolute fitness values, individuals are ranked.
  - Selection probability depends on rank rather than raw fitness score, reducing bias toward overly dominant solutions.
- **Elitism:** Ensures that the best individuals are carried over to the next generation unchanged.
  - Helps preserve high-quality solutions while allowing further improvement.

# 4.3 IMPACT OF SURVIVAL OF THE FITTEST ON GENETIC ALGORITHMS

The principle of Survival of the Fittest ensures that Genetic Algorithms effectively explore and exploit the search space. However, excessive reliance on selecting only the best individuals can lead to premature convergence, where the population loses diversity and gets stuck in a local optimum. To mitigate this, mutation is introduced, allowing for new genetic variations that may lead to better solutions.

## Parent Selection in Genetic Algorithms

### Introduction

Parent selection is a crucial step in Genetic Algorithms (GAs) where individuals are chosen to produce offspring for the next generation. This process influences the convergence rate and effectiveness of the algorithm by selecting high-quality individuals while maintaining genetic diversity.

### Importance of Parent Selection

1. **Promotes Good Solutions:** Selects individuals with higher fitness, ensuring better offspring.
2. **Maintains Diversity:** Prevents premature convergence by allowing genetic variations.
3. **Balances Exploration and Exploitation:** Ensures both new solutions and improvement of existing ones.

### Types of Parent Selection Methods

#### *1. Roulette Wheel Selection*

Also known as **Fitness Proportionate Selection**, this method assigns selection probability proportional to fitness. Higher fitness individuals have a higher chance of being selected.

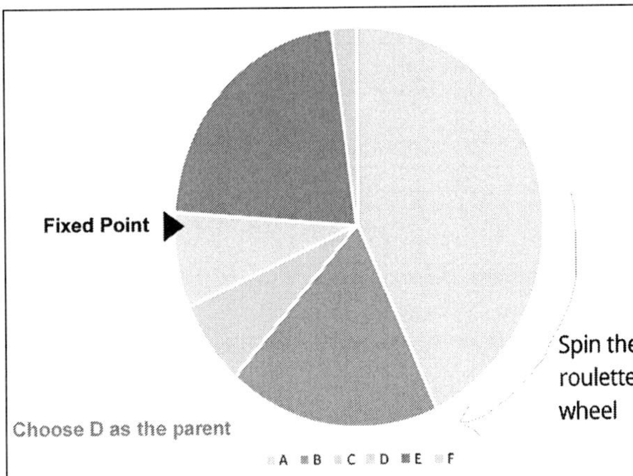


| Chromosome | Fitness Value |
|---|---|
| A | 8.2 |
| B | 3.2 |
| C | 1.4 |
| D | 1.2 |
| E | 4.2 |
| F | 0.3 |

*Fig. 4.2: Roulette Wheel Selection Roulette Wheel's*

***Table 4.3:*** *Selection Pseudo Code*

```
for all members of population
sum += fitness of this individual
end for
for all members of population
probability = sum of probabilities = (fitness/sum)
sum of probabilities += probability
end for
loop until new population is full
do this twice
number = Random between 0 and 1
for all members of population
if number > probability but less than next probability then
you have been selected
end for
end
create offspring
end loop
```

It is clear that a fitter individual has a greater pie on the wheel and therefore a greater chance of landing in front of the fixed point when the wheel is rotated. Therefore, the probability of choosing an individual depends directly on its fitness.

Implementation wise, the following steps are:

Calculate S = the sum of a finesses.

Generate a random number between 0 and S.

Starting from the top of the population, keep adding the finesses to the partial sum P, till P<S.

The individual for which P exceeds S is the chosen individual.

**Example:**

Assume the following population and fitness values:

| Individual | Fitness | Selection Probability |
|---|---|---|
| A | 5 | 5 / 21 = 0.238 |
| B | 8 | 8 / 21 = 0.381 |
| C | 3 | 3 / 21 = 0.143 |
| D | 5 | 5 / 21 = 0.238 |

### *2. Tournament Selection*

A subset of individuals is randomly selected, and the best individual is chosen as a parent. Larger tournament sizes increase selection pressure.

### *3. Rank-Based Selection*

Individuals are ranked based on fitness, and selection probabilities are assigned based on rank rather than fitness values, preventing dominance of high-fitness individuals.

### *4. Elitism Selection*

A portion of the best individuals is directly copied to the next generation, ensuring that high-quality solutions are preserved.

## 4.4 ALGORITHM FOR PARENT SELECTION

1. **Evaluate Fitness:** Compute fitness scores for all individuals.
2. **Assign Selection Probabilities:** Based on the chosen method (e.g., roulette wheel, rank-based).
3. **Select Parents:** Choose individuals based on probabilities or tournament rules.
4. **Return Selected Parents:** Proceed with crossover and mutation.

### Fitness Computations in Genetic Algorithms

Fitness computation is a crucial step in Genetic Algorithms (GAs) that determines the quality of candidate solutions in solving a given problem. It plays a significant role in guiding the evolutionary process by evaluating individuals based on predefined criteria and selecting the best-performing ones for reproduction.

### Understanding Fitness Computation

In Genetic Algorithms, each individual (chromosome) represents a potential solution to the problem. The fitness function is a mathematical function that quantifies how well an individual performs relative to others in the population. Higher fitness values indicate better solutions.

Fitness computation influences:

- **Selection:** Higher fitness individuals have a better chance of being selected for crossover.
- **Evolutionary Progress:** Ensures that over generations, the population improves in quality.
- **Convergence:** Helps the algorithm move toward an optimal or near-optimal solution.

### Types of Fitness Functions

Fitness functions are problem-specific and designed according to the nature of the optimization task. The common types include:

#### Maximization Problems

Used when the goal is to maximize a certain objective.

**Example:** Maximizing profit in an investment portfolio.

Maximization Problem – Investment Portfolio Optimization

| Stock | Expected Return (%) | Allocation (%) |
|---|---|---|
| A | 10 | 30 |
| B | 12 | 40 |
| C | 8 | 30 |

#### *Fitness Computation*

F(x) = (10 × 0.30) + (12 × 0.40) + (8 × 0.30) = 3 + 4.8 + 2.4 = 10.2

Thus, the fitness score of this solution is **10.2% return**.

### Minimization Problems

Used when the objective is to minimize a cost or error.

**Example:** Reducing the total distance in a traveling salesman problem.

Minimization Problem – Traveling Salesman Problem (TSP)

| Route Segment | Distance (km) |
|---|---|
| A → B | 10 |
| B → C | 15 |
| C → D | 20 |
| D → A | 25 |

Total Distance:

$D(x) = 10 + 15 + 20 + 25 = 70$

Fitness Computation:

$F(x) = 1 / 70 = 0.0143$

Thus, the fitness score of this route is **0.0143**.

## Constraint-Based Problems

Involves penalty functions for solutions that violate constraints.

**Example:** Optimizing resource allocation while adhering to budget constraints.

Constraint-Based Problem – Employee Scheduling

| Shift | Required Workers | Assigned Workers |
|---|---|---|
| Morning | 5 | 4 |
| Evening | 6 | 7 |
| Night | 4 | 4 |

Deviation:

$(5 - 4)^2 + (6 - 7)^2 + (4 - 4)^2 = 1 + 1 + 0 = 2$

If overtime violations occur, a penalty P(x) is added.

**Final Fitness Score:**

$F(x) = -(2 + P(x))$

Negative values indicate higher scheduling errors.

### Key Considerations in Fitness Computation

- **Scalability:** The fitness function should efficiently evaluate large populations.
- **Normalization:** Fitness values should be normalized to prevent dominance of large-scale values.
- **Penalty Handling:** Constraints should be managed using penalties to ensure valid solutions.
- **Computational Complexity:** Simpler fitness functions lead to faster evaluations.

## Crossover

Crossover is a genetic operator that combines two parent solutions to produce offspring. It simulates biological reproduction, ensuring the exchange of genetic material to explore new regions in the solution space.

### Types of Crossover

#### *1. Single-Point Crossover*

In this method, a crossover point is randomly chosen in the parent chromosomes, and genetic material is swapped between them.

#### *Example*

- **Parent 1:** 11001|011
- **Parent 2:** 10110|110
- **Offspring 1:** 11001|110
- **Offspring 2:** 10110|011

#### *2. Multi-Point Crossover*

In multi-point crossover, two or more crossover points are selected, increasing variation in the offspring.

#### *Example*

- **Parent 1:** 110|010|11
- **Parent 2:** 101|110|00
- **Offspring 1:** 110|110|11
- **Offspring 2:** 101|010|00

#### *3. Uniform Crossover*

Each gene is randomly swapped between the two parents with a 50% probability, allowing for more diverse offspring.

### Algorithm for Crossover

1. Select two parent chromosomes from the population.
2. Choose a crossover point (or points).
3. Swap genetic material between parents at the selected points.
4. Generate two new offspring.
5. Return offspring for further processing.

### Crossover Example Table

| Parent 1 | Parent 2 | Crossover Type | Offspring 1 | Offspring 2 |
|---|---|---|---|---|
| 11001011 | 10110110 | Single-Point | 11001110 | 10110011 |
| 11001011 | 10110110 | Two-Point | 11010111 | 10100010 |
| 11001011 | 10110110 | Uniform | 11110110 | 10001011 |

## Mutation

Mutation is a genetic operator that introduces small random changes in chromosomes. It helps maintain genetic diversity and prevents premature convergence.

### Types of Mutation

#### *1. Bit-Flip Mutation*

A randomly selected bit in a binary string is flipped (0 to 1 or 1 to 0).

#### *Example*

- **Original:** 11001011
- **Mutated:** 11011011

#### *2. Swap Mutation*

Two positions in the chromosome are randomly swapped.

#### *Example*

- **Original:** 11001011
- **Mutated:** 11101001

#### *3. Inversion Mutation*

A subset of the chromosome is reversed.

#### *Example*

- Original: 11001011
- **Mutated:** 11010011

### Algorithm for Mutation

1. Select an individual chromosome from the population.
2. Choose a mutation rate.
3. Modify one or more genes based on the mutation type.
4. Return the mutated chromosome.

### Mutation Example Table

| Original Chromosome | Mutation Type | Mutated Chromosome |
|---|---|---|
| 11001011 | Bit-Flip | 11011011 |
| 11001011 | Swap | 11101001 |
| 11001011 | Inversion | 11010011 |

## 4.5 REPRODUCTION IN GENETIC ALGORITHMS

Reproduction is a crucial step in Genetic Algorithms (GAs) where new solutions are generated from the existing population. It ensures the propagation of high-quality solutions through selection, crossover, and mutation. The primary objective of reproduction is to create offspring that inherit desirable traits from their parents, improving the overall fitness of the population.

**Importance of Reproduction in GAs**

1. **Ensures Genetic Diversity:** Introduces new genetic variations, preventing premature convergence.
2. **Guides Optimization:** Helps refine solutions towards an optimal state by passing beneficial traits.
3. **Balances Exploration and Exploitation:** Ensures that the search space is explored while refining good solutions.

## Types of Reproduction Methods

### *1. Selection Mechanisms*

Selection is the process of choosing parents based on their fitness. Various selection methods exist, including:

***Table 4.4:*** *Comparison of Selection Methods*

| Selection Method | Description | Advantages | Disadvantages |
|---|---|---|---|
| Roulette Wheel | Probability proportional to fitness | Simple to implement | Can be biased towards high fitness |
| Tournament | Random selection of groups, best individual chosen | Works well in noisy environments | Can be computationally expensive |
| Rank-based | Selection based on rank rather than fitness | Avoids premature convergence | Slower convergence |
| Elitism | Top solutions directly passed to next generation | Ensures best solutions are retained | Can reduce diversity |

### *2. Crossover in Reproduction*

Crossover is the process of combining two parent solutions to produce offspring. It allows beneficial traits to be passed on and helps in exploring new regions of the search space.

#### *Example: Single-Point Crossover*

- **Parent 1:** 11001|011
- **Parent 2:** 10110|110
- **Offspring 1:** 11001|110
- **Offspring 2:** 10110|011

### *3. Mutation in Reproduction*

Mutation introduces random variations in offspring to maintain genetic diversity and avoid local optima. Common types of mutation include bit-flip, swap, and inversion mutations.

*Example: Bit-Flip Mutation*

- **Original:** 11001011
- **Mutated:** 11011011

### Algorithm for Reproduction

1. **Selection:** Choose parent individuals from the population based on a selection mechanism.
2. **Crossover:** Apply crossover to selected parents to generate new offspring.
3. **Mutation:** Introduce small random changes to offspring.
4. **Evaluation:** Compute fitness values for the new offspring.
5. **Replacement:** Integrate offspring into the population for the next generation.

## 4.6 RANK METHOD AND RANK SPACE METHOD IN GENETIC ALGORITHMS

Rank-based selection is a method used in Genetic Algorithms (GAs) where individuals are selected based on their rank instead of their absolute fitness values. This approach prevents the dominance of high-fitness individuals and maintains diversity in the population.

### Importance of Rank-Based Selection

1. **Prevents Premature Convergence:** Ensures weaker individuals have a fair chance of selection.
2. **Avoids Fitness Scaling Issues:** Works well in dynamic fitness landscapes.
3. **Provides Stable Selection Pressure:** Ensures a balanced evolution process.

### Algorithm for Rank Method

- **Evaluate Fitness:** Compute the fitness values of all individuals in the population.
- **Rank Individuals:** Sort the population in increasing or decreasing order of fitness. Assign rank 1 to the worst and N (total population size) to the best individual.
- **Assign Selection Probabilities:** Compute selection probabilities based on the rank rather than raw fitness values. A common formula is where P(i) is the probability of selecting the i-th individual.

$$P(i) = \frac{\text{Rank}(i)}{\sum_{J=1}^{N} \text{Rank}(j)}$$

- **Perform Selection:** Use a selection mechanism (e.g., roulette wheel) to choose parents based on the computed probabilities.
- **Proceed to Crossover & Mutation:** Selected parents undergo crossover and mutation to generate offspring for the next generation.

### Rank Method

In the Rank Method, individuals are sorted based on their fitness values and assigned a rank. Selection probabilities are then distributed based on ranks rather than raw fitness scores.

### Example: Rank Method Calculation

Consider the following population with their fitness values:

| Individual | Fitness | Rank | Selection Probability |
|---|---|---|---|
| A | 20 | 4 | 4 / 10 = 0.4 |
| B | 15 | 3 | 3 / 10 = 0.3 |
| C | 10 | 2 | 2 / 10 = 0.2 |
| D | 5 | 1 | 1 / 10 = 0.1 |

## Rank Space Method in Genetic Algorithms

The Rank Space Method is an advanced variation of the Rank Method used in Genetic Algorithms (GAs). It assigns selection probabilities based on an individual's rank while allowing non-linear distribution of selection pressure. Unlike the standard rank-based selection, which uses linear ranking, the Rank Space Method applies exponential, power-law, or other nonlinear distributions to control selection intensity.

## Algorithm for Rank Space Method

- **Evaluate Fitness:** Compute the fitness values of all individuals in the population.
- **Rank Individuals:** Sort the population based on fitness, assigning rank = 1 to the lowest fitness and rank = N to the highest fitness.
- **Assign Rank:** Based Selection Probabilities Using a Nonlinear Function:

A commonly used formula is exponential ranking

where r(i) is the rank of the i-th individual.

- **Selection Process:** Use a selection technique like Roulette Wheel Selection or Stochastic Universal Sampling (SUS) based on the computed probabilities.
- **Proceed to Crossover and Mutation:** Selected parents undergo crossover and mutation to generate offspring for the next generation.

## Step-by-step Calculation

**Sorting & Assigning Ranks:** Higher fitness → Higher rank.

### Exponential Probability Assignment

Compute eranke$^{\{rank\}}$(or $e^{rank}$) for each individual.

**Sum of all exponentiated ranks:** 148.41 + 54.60 + 20.09 + 7.39 + 2.71 = 208.19148.41 + 54.60 + 20.09 + 7.39 + 2.71 = 208.19148.41+ 54.60 + 20.09 + 7.39 + 2.71 = 208.19.

### Normalize Probabilities

P(A) = 148.41/208.19 = 0.713P(A) = 148.41 / 208.19 = 0.713P(A)=148.41/208.19=0.713

P(B) = 54.60/208.19 = 0.262P(B) = 54.60 / 208.19 = 0.262P(B)=54.60/208.19=0.262

P(C) = 20.09/208.19 = 0.097P(C) = 20.09 / 208.19 = 0.097P(C)=20.09/208.19=0.097

P(D) = 7.39/208.19 = 0.035P(D) = 7.39 / 208.19 = 0.035P(D)=7.39/208.19=0.035

P(E) = 2.71/208.19 = 0.013P(E) = 2.71 / 208.19 = 0.013P(E)=2.71/208.19=0.013

These probabilities determine the likelihood of each individual being selected as a parent.

## Example Calculation for Rank Space Method

| Individual | Fitness | Rank | Exponential Probability Calculation | Normalized Probability |
|---|---|---|---|---|
| A | 25 | 5 | $e^5 = 148.41$ | 148.41 / 208.19 = 0.713 |
| B | 18 | 4 | $e^4 = 54.60$ | 54.60 / 208.19 = 0.262 |
| C | 12 | 3 | $e^3 = 20.09$ | 20.09 / 208.19 = 0.097 |
| D | 8 | 2 | $e^2 = 7.39$ | 7.39 / 208.19 = 0.035 |
| E | 5 | 1 | $e^1 = 2.71$ | 2.71 / 208.19 = 0.013 |

## Advantages of Rank Space Method

- **Enhances Selection Pressure:** Gives greater preference to higher-ranked individuals compared to linear rank-based selection.
- **Provides Nonlinear Control:** Different functions (e.g., exponential, power-law) can be used to adjust selection intensity.
- **Maintains Diversity:** Ensures that lower-ranked individuals still have some chance of selection.

# Swarm Intelligence

**5** **UNIT**

## 5.1 PARTICLE SWARM OPTIMIZATION (PSO)

### 5.1.1 Introduction to PSO

Particle Swarm Optimization (PSO) is a population-based metaheuristic optimization algorithm inspired by the social behavior of birds and fish. It was developed by James Kennedy and Russell Eberhart in 1995. PSO is widely used in solving complex optimization problems due to its simplicity, efficiency, and ability to converge quickly.

In PSO, a group of candidate solutions, called particles, moves through the solution space by following simple rules derived from their personal experiences and the collective experience of the swarm. Each particle updates its position and velocity based on its best-found solution and the best-found solution of its neighbors or the entire swarm.

### Representation in Genetic Algorithms

- **Swarm:** A collection of particles (candidate solutions).
- **Particle:** An individual solution in the swarm.
- **Velocity:** The direction and speed at which a particle moves.
- **Position:** The current solution represented by a particle.
- **Personal Best (pBest):** The best solution a particle has encountered.
- **Global Best (gBest):** The best solution found by the entire swarm.

  The velocity update rule given by:

$$v_i(t + 1) = wv_i(t) + c_1r_1(pBesti - x_i) + c_2r_2(gBest - x_i)$$

where:

- *vi(t)* is the velocity of particle i at iteration t.
- *w* is the inertia weight, balancing exploration and exploitation.
- $c_1$, $c_2$ are cognitive and social coefficients.
- $r_1$, $r_2$ are random numbers between 0 and 1.
- *pBest*, is the best position found by particle *i*.
- *gBest* is the best position found by the entire swarm.

### 5.1.2 Types of PSO: Global and Local

#### 1. Global PSO (gBest Model)

Global PSO follows a topology where all particles share information with every other particle. This means that each particle is influenced by the best solution found by the entire swarm.

### Characteristics of Global PSO

Faster convergence because particles quickly move towards the global best.

Can get trapped in local optima, especially in multimodal optimization problems.

Less diversity in the swarm over time.

Equation for Global PSO:

The velocity update in global PSO uses the best solution found by the entire swarm:

$$v_i(t + 1) = wv_i(t) + c_1r_1(pBesti - x_i) + c_2r_2(gBest - x_i)$$

where gBest is determined by considering all particles in the swarm.

### Example of Global PSO

Consider optimizing the Rastrigin function, a common test function in optimization:

$$f(x) = 10n + \sum_{i=1}^{n}[x_i^2 - 10\cos(2\pi x_i)]$$

Using global PSO, the swarm quickly converges towards the global minimum (which occurs at $x = 0$ \). However, in a complex landscape, it may get stuck in local optima.

### Local PSO (Best Model)

Local PSO uses a toplogy where each particle only shares informatin with a subset of neighbors rather than the entire swarm.

### Characteristics of Local PSO

- Slower convergence but better exploration.
- Less prone to premature convergence, making it useful for complex and multimodal problems.
- Maintains higher diversity in the swarm, improving the chance of escaping local optima.

### Equation for Local PSO

The velocity update in local PSO considers the best solution found within a neighborhood of particles. The equation is:

$$v_i(t + 1) = wv_i(t) + c_1r_1(pBest_i - x_i) + c_2r_2(IBest - x_i)$$

where IBest is the best solution found by a small group of neighboring particles rather than the entire swarm.

$$v_i(t + 1) = wv_i(t) + c_1r_1(pBest_i - x_i) + c_2r_2(IBest - x_i)$$

### Example of Local PSO

In the Traveling Salesman Problem (TSP), local PSO is often more effective than global PSO. Since TSP has a highly nonlinear solution space, local PSO ensures better exploration and avoids premature convergence, leading to improved solutions over time.

*Table 5.1: Comparison Between Global and Local PSO*

| Feature | Global PSO | Local PSO |
|---|---|---|
| Convergence Speed | Faster | Slower |
| Exploration | Lower | Higher |
| Exploitation | Higher | Lower |
| Risk of Local Optima | Higher | Lower |
| Communication | Global | Limited to neighbors |

### Hybrid PSO Approaches

To leverage the advantages of both models, researchers have developed hybrid approaches such as:

- **Adaptive PSO:** Dynamically adjusts inertia weight and neighborhood size.
- **Multi-Swarm PSO:** Uses multiple swarms, each with different strategies.
- **Quantum PSO:** Incorporates quantum mechanics principles for enhanced exploration.

### Real-World Applications of PSO

Engineering Design Optimization: Used in aerodynamics, robotics, and structural optimization.

- **Medical Image Processing:** Used for segmentation, classification, and feature selection.
- **Financial Forecasting:** Applied in stock market prediction and portfolio optimization.
- **Machine Learning and AI:** Helps in hyperparameter tuning and feature selection.

## 5.2 INTRODUCTION TO ANT COLONY OPTIMIZATION (ACO)

Ant Colony Optimization (ACO) is a swarm intelligence-based metaheuristic algorithm inspired by the foraging behavior of ants. Proposed by Marco Dorigo in the early 1990s, ACO is widely used for solving combinatorial optimization problems, including routing, scheduling, and network design.

ACO is based on how real ants find the shortest path between their nest and food sources. Ants deposit pheromones on paths, reinforcing shorter routes. This emergent behavior allows ACO algorithms to effectively search for optimal solutions in complex problem spaces.

### Key Components of ACO

1. **Artificial Ants:** Agents that explore the solution space.
2. **Pheromone Trails:** Virtual chemical markers used to guide the search.
3. **Visibility (Heuristic Information):** A measure of problem-specific desirability (e.g., inverse of distance in routing problems).

4. **Exploration and Exploitation:** Balancing randomness and pheromone-based guidance.
5. **Evaporation:** Gradual reduction of pheromone levels to prevent premature convergence.

## ACO Algorithm

1. **Initialize Parameters:** Set pheromone levels, heuristic information, and algorithm parameters (α, β, ρ).
2. **Construct Solutions:** Each ant builds a solution step by step based on a probabilistic rule.

Construct Solutions:

- Each ant builds a solution step by step based on a probabillistic rule:

$$P_{ij} = \frac{r_{ij}^{\alpha} \cdot \eta_{ij}^{\beta}}{\sum_{k \varepsilon N} t_{ik}^{\alpha} \cdot \eta_{ik}^{\beta}}$$

where:

- Tij is the pheromove value for edge (i, j).
- $\eta_{ij}$ is the heuristic value (e.g., 1/distance).
- $\alpha$ controls the influence of pheromone.

↓

- $\beta$ controls the influnce of heuristic information.

3. **Update Pheromone Levels:** After all ants construct their solutions, pheromones are updated.

- After all ants construct their solutions, phermones are updated:

$$T_{ij} = (1 - p)T_{ij} + \sum_{k} T_{ij}^{k}$$

where p is the evaporation rate, and $\Delta T_{ij}^{k}$ is the pheromone deposited by ant *k*.

4. Repeat Until Stopping Condition is Met (e.g., max iterations or convergence).

**Example:** Solving the Traveling Salesman Problem (TSP) with ACO

The TSP requires finding the shortest possible route visiting a set of cities exactly once and returning to the starting point. ACO effectively solves TSP by modeling it as a graph and using pheromone trails to reinforce shorter paths.

### Example Problem

Consider 4 cities with the following distance matrix:

| | A | B | C | D |
|---|---|---|---|---|
| A | 0 | 10 | 15 | 20 |
| B | 10 | 0 | 35 | 25 |
| C | 15 | 35 | 0 | 30 |
| D | 20 | 25 | 30 | 0 |

### *Step 1: Initialize Parameters*

- $\alpha = 1, \beta = 2, \rho = 0.5$
- Initial pheromone levels set equally.

### *Step 2: Ants Construct Solutions*

Each ant selects the next city based on the probability formula. Suppose an ant starts at A, it calculates probabilities for moving to B, C, or D based on pheromone values and distances.

### *Step 3: Update Pheromone Levels*

After all ants complete a tour, pheromone values are updated using:

$$T_{ij} = (1 - p)Tij + \sum_{k} \frac{Q}{L_k}$$

where $Q$ is a constant and $L_k$ is the total tour length of ant $k$.

### *Step 4: Repeat Until Convergence*

The process repeats for multiple iterations, refining the pheromone trails and converging to an optimal path (e.g., A → B → D → C → A with total distance = 80).

### Applications of ACO

1. **Network Routing:** Dynamic path selection in telecommunications and logistics.
2. **Job Scheduling:** Optimizing production and resource allocation.
3. **Robotics:** Path planning for autonomous robots.
4. **Bio informatics:** Sequence alignment and protein structure prediction.

## 5.3 MAX-MIN ANT SYSTEM FOR FEATURE SELECTION IN LOGISTIC REGRESSION

Feature selection plays a crucial role in improving the efficiency and accuracy of machine learning models. In classification tasks such as logistic regression, selecting the most relevant features enhances performance while reducing computational complexity. Traditional feature selection methods, such as filter, wrapper, and embedded approaches, often face limitations in handling high-dimensional data. Swarm intelligence-based techniques, such as Ant Colony Optimization (ACO) and its variant, Max-Min Ant System (MMAS), provide effective solutions for feature selection by simulating the collective foraging behavior of ants.

### 5.3.1 ACO and Its Variants

Ant Colony Optimization (ACO) is a metaheuristic algorithm inspired by the way ants find the shortest path between their nest and a food source. ACO involves:

- **Pheromone Trails:** Ants deposit pheromones to communicate information about optimal paths.
- **Exploration and Exploitation:** Probability-based selection of paths to balance exploration and exploitation.
- **Updating Pheromone Values:** Reinforcing beneficial solutions while evaporating outdated information.

Max-Min Ant System (MMAS) is an improved version of ACO designed to control pheromone values and prevent premature convergence by restricting pheromone deposition within predefined maximum and minimum bounds.

## 3.3.2 Feature Selection Using MMAS

- **Feature Representation:** Each feature in the dataset is treated as a possible selection in the feature subset.
- **Pheromone Initialization:** Assign initial pheromone values to all features, ensuring uniform exploration at the start.
- **Ant Population Setup:** Define the number of artificial ants used in the optimization process.
- **Parameter Settings:** Configure MMAS parameters such as number of ants, pheromone levels, evaporation rate, and number of iterations.

Each ant constructs a feature subset by probabilistically selecting features based on pheromone influence and heuristic information.

## 5.3.3 Model Evaluation Using Logistic Regression

Train logistic regression with the selected feature subset and evaluate performance using accuracy, AUC-ROC, and F1-score.

After evaluating the logistic regression model, pheromone values are updated based on performance.

MMAS stops when the maximum number of iterations is reached, or no significant improvement occurs.

### Advantages of MMAS in Feature Selection

- **Efficient Exploration:** MMAS prevents early stagnation by regulating pheromone deposition.
- **Feature Subset Optimization:** Ensures that only relevant features are selected.
- **Avoids Overfitting:** Selects a balanced number of features.
- **Scalability:** Works well with high-dimensional datasets.

### Challenges and Limitations

- **Computational Cost:** MMAS is computationally expensive for very large datasets.
- **Parameter Sensitivity:** Proper tuning of $\alpha$, $\beta$, $\rho$, and pheromone bounds is required.
- **Local Optima:** MMAS may still get stuck in suboptimal feature subsets.

### Experimental Evaluation

- Use benchmark datasets for classification tasks.
- Compare MMAS-selected features against other feature selection techniques.
- Assess performance using accuracy, precision, recall, and computational time.